# 40 Days at a Dumpster

"*40 Days at a Dumpster* by Pam Van Dop is a beautifully written and courageous work that powerfully reminds us that God is present in our struggles and that we can trust him through every season of life. Pam's intimate journey through her wrestle with God invites readers into a profound healing experience, fostering a deeper connection with the Lord. It's a compelling read that will touch the hearts of many."

—NICOLE LANGMAN, author of *You Are Wanted: Reclaiming the Truth of Who You Are*

**PRAISE FOR THE FIRST EDITION:**

"In a church culture that is hemorrhaging 'the faithful,' we need to tap into the experience of those who dared ask the questions and have come out the other side! Pam writes about her experience of going back to the genesis of her big pain to find God and ask the haunting questions she had lived with for decades. Her experience with grace and the understanding of what it truly is will leave you hope-filled and expectant. Pam is a brilliant writer, and you may just find yourself sitting right beside her on this journey."

—EDEN JERSAK, co-author of *Rivers from Eden*

"Pam Van Dop's account of her prayer/healing journey, twenty years after her deep wounding, teems with evocative, pastoral reflections. *40 Days at a Dumpster* seamlessly weaves together longings for the Lord's gracious presence, remembered trauma, biblical wisdom, encouragement from others, and brief teachings from wise Christian elders as it narrates its six-week passage. There are more folks in all of our social circles with similar experiences than meet the eye; consequently, there are blessings here for every reader."

—SYD HIELEMA, Director of Connections Project, CRCNA

"While this is Pam's journey, it reiterates the process of transformation we all must take at some time. Her wrestling between faith and her mental wellbeing is a vital message for us all, especially that faith and mental wellness are not mutually exclusive. Often our journey to emotional healing is rugged and rough—pieces of us get chipped off, cut and torn, scraped, and bloody. But, as she so clearly shares, we are not alone in that struggle and transformation. Jesus walks with us, lovingly prodding, nudging, revealing, and encouraging us."

—ALLEN KLEINE DETERS, Pastor Care Coordinator, Agora Network Ministries

"What if we aren't as fine with it as we hoped we were? *40 Days at a Dumpster* is a deeply honest, no-holds-barred look at the way we interact with pain, suffering, and disappointment with God. This book is candid without sensationalizing the deepest, most vulnerable thoughts and questions that many of us have had about our own lives but dared not express. Pam shows us how to scratch that itch we can't reach, and she cuts through our religious conditioning with a firm but gentle hand. Pam is a trustworthy guide as she invites us to join her on a transformative journey of letting go, embracing mystery, and rising to find the new life Jesus promised us."

—KARINA LOEWEN, Co-host of *We Should Record This* podcast

# 40 Days at a Dumpster

*Finding Healing and Grace in the Garbage*

*Second Edition*

PAM VAN DOP

RESOURCE *Publications* • Eugene, Oregon

40 DAYS AT A DUMPSTER
Finding Healing and Grace in the Garbage, Second Edition

Copyright © 2025 Pam Van Dop. All rights reserved. Except for brief quotations in critical publications or reviews, no part of this book may be reproduced in any manner without prior written permission from the publisher. Write: Permissions, Wipf and Stock Publishers, 199 W. 8th Ave., Suite 3, Eugene, OR 97401.

Resource Publications
An Imprint of Wipf and Stock Publishers
199 W. 8th Ave., Suite 3
Eugene, OR 97401

www.wipfandstock.com

PAPERBACK ISBN: 979-8-3852-6375-2
HARDCOVER ISBN: 979-8-3852-6376-9
EBOOK ISBN: 979-8-3852-6377-6

12/08/25

Excerpts from The Solace of Fierce Landscapes by Beldon C Lane. Copyright © 1998 by Beldon C Lane. Reproduced with permission of the Oxford University Press through PLSclear.

Unless otherwise noted, Scripture quotations are taken from THE HOLY BIBLE, NEW INTERNATIONAL VERSION®, NIV.® Copyright © 1973, 1978, 1984, 2011 by Biblica, Inc.® Used by permission. All rights reserved worldwide.

For my husband,

Nolan,

who walks beside me and supports me

always and forever.

# Contents

*Introduction: The Challenge* — ix
**Week 1**  God's Presence — 1
**Week 2**  Shame — 20
**Week 3**  Healing — 34
**Week 4**  Finding Grace — 47
**Week 5**  Grace—The Finality of Life — 60
**Week 6**  Grace—The Finality of Death — 71
*Bibliography* — 83

# INTRODUCTION

# The Challenge

SHOULDERS SLUMPED, I PRESSED my back against the cold metal of the dumpster and slowly slid down to sit on the concrete. Looking around, I was rattled by just how uninviting the alley was. When I chose this specific spot, I was unaware of the unappealing details: the nauseating smell of the garbage, the sounds of metal scraping against metal, the sludge near my feet that had been accumulating over months, and the shadows that played with my mind. I scoffed at my decision to spend time with God in this place. Really, it was a ridiculous idea. I had been in a similar place, and God's presence was the last thing that I remember. My experiences had taught me that a place like this brings pain, abuse, and humiliation. To willingly sit here and wait for a personal God to show up, made my stomach twist into a knot. I came with very low expectations.

Two weeks previous, I stood at the pulpit of my church and challenged the congregation to ask God their big questions and wait for answers. It was the end of June, and I explained to them that as the school and ministry year was coming to an end, this could be the perfect time to explore some questions they had about their faith. Was God real? Could God be trusted? Where was God when life was tough? Why doesn't God fix the brokenness? It was meant to encourage the church to make their faith real and relevant.

## INTRODUCTION: THE CHALLENGE

For some reason, I thought this could be helpful for others, but believed the brick walls I encountered doing such an exercise myself were permanent structures. I had desperately cried out to God numerous times for answers and explanations— only to be met with the sound of air. I had heard other people's stories and read their books of when they heard the voice of God, convincing me that God does, on occasion, answer. But I had already been convinced, whether it was my arrogance or avoidance, that I was exempt. God had shown me His indifference to my big questions a long time ago, so I thought this advice didn't apply to me. I fully believed that God was willing to meet others, so I blessed them on their journeys. I resorted to sitting alone on the bench, cheering everyone on from the sidelines.

But then my pastor said something similar in his sermon the next Sunday. He phrased it differently, but it was the same challenge: "Find time this week to sit with God. Set aside some time and sit in His presence." There were to be no questions, no petitions, no demands, not even well-meaning bargains or negotiations. It was to be a time of *being*, instead of *doing*. Out loud, I knew it was a friendly challenge to the congregation, but into my ears and down to my heart, it was an order. The words had found a secret way in, dodged all my excuses, found my weakened soul, and nudged it to attention.

I was a house divided. My heart yearned for this experience of sitting with God, yet my head scoffed at how it seemed like a romanticized idea. My heart broke open a little, begging sheepishly to try one more time. My head shouted out cynicism and skepticism at the empty venture.

To be honest, I knew I could easily set up a perfect place for God to meet me. I could set the table for the honored guest through a worship service, or a prayer night, or even a nature walk. I could provide the place, the right atmosphere, and a simple prayer asking Him to grace me with His presence, and He would show up. I could pour myself a cup of coffee, shut my eyes, and breathe in God's presence in the freshly roasted coffee beans. I could go to a nearby park, sit on a bench, and gaze at the mountains in their

## INTRODUCTION: THE CHALLENGE

splendor. I could feel the crisp, cool air fill my lungs, hear the distant delightful chirp of birds, and feel the peace and contentment of God wash over me. That would be nice. And God would be nice. And everything would be nice. But I grew up with a gospel of niceness and pleasantries, and I truly wondered if there was a believable gospel in the dirt and the grit. How and where does God show up in the least likely areas?

As I sat in the church pew that Sunday morning, I was scared that someone was reading my inner thoughts. I imagined into life their accusatory thoughts towards me. How dare I challenge a good God? How dare I doubt His presence in the brokenness of the world? How dare I accuse God of being two-faced: a romantic in the good, yet detached in the ugly. How dare I question the nature of a God I've followed all my life?

I came face to face with my deeply held belief that God was willing to step in and step out of my life according to His preference and that He was willing to be a part of every good and life-giving part of me, but in the same breath, perfectly content to take a step back from the difficult and soul-numbing experiences of life.

That became my test for God. I resolved to be obedient to the command to sit with God in His presence, but it would be in a place where I believed He would least likely be.

# WEEK 1

## God's Presence

I FOUND MYSELF SITTING in a back alley of a strip mall, with a single spilt pop can and several broken beer bottles next to a dumpster that smelled like urine. I set my alarm on my phone for one hour. It was all the time I could afford since my three kids were at a morning summer camp for the week, and this was my one window of time that I could set aside everything for me—and God. I sat there in silence . . . agonizing silence.

Silence can't be the right descriptor though. Because even though I was silent, the world around me was not. I heard the squeal of tires leaving a parking lot, the drone of cars driving on the street nearby. I heard footsteps which made my heart race in panic. I heard people talking, which reached my ears like whispers and murmurs I couldn't make sense of. Things around me creaked and groaned, and I couldn't figure out their source. I looked down at my hands, and they were trembling. This was too familiar in the worst kind of way. I was flooded with memories I had tried to forget for the longest time.

Twenty years ago, I graduated from high school. This past year, emails and social media posts reminded me of that fact. Questions were thrown out into the digital realm: would anyone like to plan a reunion? Wouldn't it be great to see everyone after all these years? Embedded in the replies were thoughts of anticipation, of celebration, of curiosity. Where had our class travelled? What had we accomplished? What kind of lives did we create in twenty years?

I don't have clear memories of my grade 12 graduation ceremony, but all the talk of twenty years ago did trigger the worst memory of my life. Every time someone mentioned the word twenty, my entire being transported back to a late January evening where, in the back alley of a strip mall, a man I didn't know raped me. It was cruel. It was damaging. It was messy. It was pure evil. When it was done, when I fought back and got away, when I ran for my life while he ran the other way, I collapsed on the ground next to a dumpster.

And now, twenty years later, I sat next to a similar dumpster. This was a different city, but it was an alley behind the same store chain. It was my best attempt to go to the place I felt God would least likely be. At least that was my experience. Twenty years ago, I didn't see Him there. Adam's Creator, Noah's Protector, Abraham's Provider, even the One who touched Jacob's hip —I didn't see that type of personal God. I didn't experience His love or mercy or grace in any way that night. Instead, I experienced indifference, insult, and shame. I came to test my memory and to test God. What really happened that night?

I sat in my silence and began a journey I didn't know if I was ready to take. My pastor's challenge was a call to apophatic prayer, or more commonly called Centering Prayer. It was a call not just to silence myself outwardly, but also to silence my voice within. M. Basil Pennington, a Trappist monk who spent much of his life reviving the ancient practice of Centering Prayer writes, "Centering Prayer is an opening, a response, a putting aside of all the debris that stands in the way of our being totally present to the present Lord so that he can be present to us. It is a laying aside of thoughts so that the heart can attend immediately to him."[1] My pastor had challenged me to push out all my distractions and refrain from presenting requests before God. He asked me to sit in God's presence with no agenda. But how do you enter into this apophatic state when you are used to a brain that keeps going

---

1. Jones, *Soul Shaper*, 76.

WEEK 1: GOD'S PRESENCE

like the Energizer bunny? My brain hummed full of activity: *How long has this dumpster been here? How long has the rusting trailer been resting here? Will I meet anyone here? I should have a carefully crafted answer for if someone approaches me. How should I frame that response? I should get groceries after I'm done here. We are out of chicken. Should I prepare the barbeque for tonight or not? I wonder if I should arrange playdates for my kids for the afternoon. No, I miss them already. I will play a board game with them. Now that summer is here, I should arrange some outings with my husband. Maybe dinner out with some friends? Wait, maybe I shouldn't— I might have to explain to them what I'm trying to do here. What am I doing here? Will I learn anything about God here? What happens if silence slowly erodes the remaining parts of my faith? Can someone accept the objective parts of Christianity but reject the subjective ones? Can I even make that distinction? If God is so relational, why hasn't He helped me with my hurt? Why did He abandon me that night? What happens if God forsakes me here again? On the other hand, what happens if He shows up? How does God deal with the rubble of society? How does He interact with the broken these days? Will He show up angry? Disinterested? Disappointed?*

    I found that the key to silencing my entire being was through the slow process of emptying myself. When a panicking thought came to my mind, I had to empty it. When a defiant impulse arose inside of me, ready to defend myself and attack God, I had to empty it. When memories flooded into my eyes, I had to empty it. I was amazed at how much I held inside, how much kept bubbling to the surface, how much kept coming up like a hot spring. With every thought, good or painful, I chose to carefully lay them side by side into a mental box labelled *To Forget*. I sealed the box and pushed it aside, temporarily forgetting their importance or impact in my life. I was cleaning it all out of my mind as if I was packing up my life and pushing it all on a moving truck to bring it to who knows where. As I was slowly pushing out all the broken pieces, the glass shards, the beautiful prisms, the dirty laundry, the garments of self-preservation . . . I became aware of a nothingness. A deep, dark, nothingness. It scared me.

What scared me the most was the realization that I had thrown myself into exile. Did I know I had done this? I had ordered myself to depart from my familiar land and go to a place of isolation. In "going to be alone with God," I willingly chose to break myself off from all of my securities and enter into a desert of sorts. Unintentionally, I had started my trek like Moses at Mount Sinai, and I was searching for the promised land. Belden Lane describes his experience of his process in his book *The Solace of Fierce Landscapes*. He explained Sinai to be "a place of being emptied, a place of dark and difficult beauty. It symbolized the wandering of the children of Israel, the experience of loss and the bread of hardness. [It] is a place far from home, a 'no man's land' of fire and smoke."[2] I was in exile, cut off from everything, and just like Moses at the base of Mount Sinai looking into a dark, thunderous cloud, I was walking this road all alone, and it scared me so much that waves of nausea came over me.

Forty-five minutes into my slow emptying of anything that came up in my mind, wanting to throw up next to the dumpster adding to the filth and grime of where I sat, I came face to face with the only thing left inside of me: my Wound. I had run from this all my life, and I wanted to run from it right there, but I didn't have the energy to do so. My running usually consisted of answering questions on behalf of God or finding an answer in a book that satisfied me like a sedative that would numb the wound away, or, in my worst moments, self-harm to distract me from the ache I felt inside. Sitting here in the alley, I didn't have the energy to do any of those things. I only had the energy to whisper aloud a question that arose—and surprised me—from deep inside my heart.

*Where are You?*

I asked it a couple of times. Letting the sound of it drift into the air, I wondered what would come of it. How would the oxygen and hydrogen particles react to the question? Would it burst open like a bomb and burn me right there? Or, would it slowly sink to the ground and be unnoticed in the mix of dust and dirt? But, it

---

2. Lane, *Solace of Fierce Landscapes*, 71.

## WEEK 1: GOD'S PRESENCE

did neither. It seemed to linger in front of me, echoing out in the stillness around me: *Where are You, God?*

Then it was quiet. Deafeningly quiet.

I looked around and realized how stupid and unsafe this idea was. First of all, I hadn't told anyone where I was going. Secondly, this place seemed like the perfect spot for any crime: theft, assault, or even murder. There was no safety here, and I had the audacity to call out to a God that had abandoned me in this same situation before. The question started as a cheeky challenge of wondering if God would show up by this dumpster, but it grew in magnitude and importance with every second that went by on my ticking timer. To a God who is and who was and who is to come, to a God that transcends timelines, this question became not only *where are You* by this dumpster today, but *where were You that night twenty years ago*, and *where will You be when I have more brokenness to endure? Where are You? Where are You?* I kept repeating it.

My heart sank as I realized this was a question of trust. *If I couldn't trust You to be there and show Yourself then and if I can't trust that You will meet me here now, how can I trust walking away from this place with any sort of confirmation that I would have God by my side in the future?* I know that I have believed in God my whole life, but I couldn't say for sure that I had *trusted* him in the heartache for that long. Could I trust that God would show up now? Life circumstances screamed at me a very loud, *No!*

But, what was I expecting in this remote place? What had I been looking for in the middle of my loneliness? In my search for God in the shameful places, what was I expecting to find? Gold panners know what they are looking for. Tornado chasers know what to chase. Miners know what to unearth. What God was I expecting as an answer to my question?

The reality is, I was looking for the God of the good places, the God that finds me when I feel secure, loved, wanted, and worth my keep in this world. I know this God. His presence feels like warmth from the sun on a summer day, like a blanket of security on a fall day, like a sip of hot chocolate warming my throat and chest on a winter day, like the smell of fresh flowers emerging from the earth on an early spring day. I was looking for a God that would be happy to sit with me and watch the calm sunset.

However, I wasn't watching a sun dip below the horizon, I was watching a tornado tear through my emotions and churn up everything I thought had been put in place. I was in crisis mode, where the code red was called and every emotion and thought in my body was scrambling for safety and life. I was in a war zone where I was tripping over land mines and shrapnel from years past that were flying at me faster than I could avoid the hits. I wanted the safe God who would be a tornado shelter, a drug to put in my IV, a rescue squad who would take me away from all the pain.

Here at the dumpster, I was looking around for someone to walk up to me and be the angel of the Lord in disguise. I wanted a homeless person to walk up to me and passionately speak of God's love and tender heart toward me. I was looking for a finger to write, on the side of the green waste bin, the confirmation of His presence and His guiding hand in my life. I wanted to be able to snap a picture to capture the miracle and prove to everyone who doubted that I had seen God's hand, that He gave me a message of love and acceptance. I was looking for a policeman to sit next to me, let me know he had been sent by God to find me at this exact place to pronounce that my dead case number was reopened, the guy who created such pain was found, justice had been served, and I could find the closure I needed for that part of my life.

In the book of Job in the Bible, Job lost everything. Seriously *everything*. Imagine finding out all in one day that your possessions, your business, and your employees were all stolen or killed. And while you were trying to process that huge blow, someone came to tell you that a house collapsed on your family. I can hardly begin to understand the hurt of Job. In fact, I can hardly process the heartache of what happens around me today, with cancer diagnoses, fatal car accidents, marriages falling apart, estranged family members. But, imagine losing everything in one day! It's unbelievable. Then, Job himself became so sick that he looked like he was on the brink of death. This takes suffering to a whole other level. Job's friends came along and tried to encourage him, tried

## WEEK 1: GOD'S PRESENCE

to explain away the pain, tried to show him how to make life better again—but they just poured salt on an open wound. Job cried out to God to intervene, to say something, at least to show up for goodness sake! I found myself echoing Job's words in desperation:

> But if I go east, he is not there;
> if I go west, I do not find him.
> When he is at work in the north, I do not see him;
> when he turns to the south, I catch no glimpse of him . . .
> But he stands alone, and who can oppose him?
> He does whatever he pleases.
> He carries out his decree against me,
> and many such plans he still has in store.
> That is why I am terrified before him;
> When I think of all this, I fear him.
> God has made my heart faint;
> the Almighty has terrified me.
> Yet I am not silenced by the darkness,
> by the thick darkness that covers my face.[3]

Job desperately asked God to show up. But, he wanted God to show up in a particular way. He wanted God to be his defence lawyer, to talk to his friends about their unfair accusations, about their lack of compassion, of their misunderstandings of why he was suffering. Job wanted God to show up as a judge, to see the case for and against him to explain the suffering of his blameless, God-focused life. But God never came that way, and he left Job in the thick darkness.

After reading 38 agonizing chapters of awkward interchange between Job and his friends, when God did show up, he didn't even answer most of the questions. God didn't go to a courtroom, he didn't look at the evidence, he didn't even address Job's so-called friends. God showed up in an entirely different way—the way Job didn't realize that he needed.

Sitting next to the dumpster, day one passed, and I found no answers. Day two came, and the hour I had set on my timer was almost done. No God today either. I felt dejected. What was the

---

3. Job 23:8–9, 13–17.

point of all this? It brought up the same shy questions from within me. I wondered what I was looking for. Who was I expecting? Like Job, was I expecting God to be something in particular?

Again, the resounding answer was *yes*. I was looking for God to reveal his presence around me and make everything right in an instant. I wanted Him to show up as the great Healer and take away my wounds that cut so deeply. I wanted a burning bush, a talking donkey, pigs running into rivers, lights striking me blind.[4] I wanted hard proof that God was there and was going to make right every wrong I felt for the last twenty years.

Or maybe I wanted Him to sit beside me and erase my memory. I wanted to forget the hurt, forget the night, forget the act, forget the words spoken, forget it all. That was the only miracle I was looking for. Where was my miracle worker? Where was He here? Where was He there?

Then, like a scene from *A Christmas Carol*,[5] I felt like I was being taken back to that night. I was looking into the alley, looking from a place outside of myself, from a vantage point I was unable to see from twenty years ago. I saw the bricks of the wall where I was pinned. I saw the dirt scuffed away on the ground where the violent interchange happened. I saw a light post cast eerie shadows that made the man look larger than he was. And then, surprisingly I saw the silhouette of another person.

Somehow I found Him in my memory. God was in the shadows. He was standing in the darkness. He was there. Why didn't I ever see him there? There was so much going on that night, so many thoughts were bombarding my brain, erasing my emotions, and numbing my body. My survival instinct was fighting back, and my head was going through overload. If so much of the night was a blur, no wonder I hadn't the eyes to look for anyone else. I couldn't. I didn't know that He was there.

The shock of His presence shook and angered me as I sat on the concrete leaned up against the dumpster. I wasn't expecting Him to be anywhere in my memory of that night—and definitely

---

4. Exod 3:2, Num 22:28, Mark 5:13, Acts 9:3.
5. Dickens, *Christmas Carol*.

## WEEK 1: GOD'S PRESENCE

not to be there like that. I thought His silence meant absence. Instead, I became aware that inwardly and outwardly, the silence was saturated with His presence. He was in the shadows, in the air that I seemed to choke down in between sobs, in the echoes of the brick walls, in the vapor of my breath. He was in my silenced voice inside of me, in the shattered heart within me, filling the void chamber of self-worth in my soul. All of the places I would have described as abandoned held a presence that I had never recognized before. You would think it would be relieving to finally find Him there, but it wasn't. It broke me even more.

My alarm buzzed, signalling the end of my hour allotment of time. I couldn't have run to my van any faster. I was glad to escape the dumpster for the day—to run from the revelation I just had. I welcomed the opportunity to distract my mind by picking up my kids, making lunch, playing at the park, doing laundry, and putting dishes away.

It was on day three and four at the dumpster that I gathered the courage to question God. I asked, *"Why?"* I was surprised at how my voice could only manage a whisper, yet it seemed to echo off the bricks of the wall I was facing while sitting on the pavement. I wasn't inquiring why God hadn't stopped the event from unfolding. I was asking Him a simpler question: *Why were You there? You saw it all. You watched. The thing is, when I didn't think You were there, it was easy to say it was all a bad dream. No one else saw what happened. No one else witnessed it.* The only thing outside of my own experience that validated that it occurred was the empty police file with no leads and no conclusion. If a tree falls in a forest and no one is there, does it make a sound? If a girl gets hurt in an alley and no one is there, did it happen? For twenty years, I was convincing myself that it was just a nightmare, that it was a bad dream, that it didn't happen.

But, the fact that God was there changed all of that. It meant there was a witness. It meant it did happen. It meant I had to stop pretending that it didn't break me.

It did break me. For the rest of my grade 12 year, I spent countless hours blaming myself for what had happened. I blamed myself for walking in the wrong place at the wrong time, for engaging in conversation with this man when he got off the bus two blocks before the alley, for somehow believing I must have done something to invite the behavior towards me. But, no amount of finger-pointing at myself changed what the experience itself told me. Rape told me that I was not special, that I was inconsequential, that I was a nobody, that I was worth nothing more than to be left by a dumpster to die. That night broke my understanding of my worth in this world. Finding out that God was there that January night didn't help to take away the pain of the experience. It made me feel even more ashamed of myself than I had ever felt before.

In the Bible, when Adam and Eve believed the lies that Satan had planted in their minds, when they chose to eat the fruit of the tree anyway, when they chose to do things their way instead of God's way, the Bible says the "eyes of both of them were opened and they realized they were naked; so they sewed fig leaves together and made coverings for themselves."[6]

I had always understood this verse at an intellectual level. Since they had disobeyed God, they realized the consequence of their actions and they were thus filled with shame. They no longer felt completely fulfilled by God, but they felt like they were lacking. They hated that feeling, they were confused at that feeling, and they hid from God because of that feeling. Further, the Bible says, "The man and his wife heard the sound of the Lord God as he was walking in the garden in the cool of the day and they hid from the Lord God among the trees of the garden."[7] They hid because of their shame—and it wasn't because of what they looked like. It was because they were ashamed that they didn't completely trust God anymore.

The explanation rolled out of my mind simple enough, but I understood the emotions, the feelings, the gut-wrenching reality that Adam and Eve went through. I sat on the ground by the dumpster and said out loud, *"I would rather that You had not been there at all than to have seen what happened to me. No one else in*

---

6. Gen 3:7.
7. Gen 3:8.

## WEEK 1: GOD'S PRESENCE

the world saw it, no one else in the world knows the truth of my dirtiness and shame and what was robbed from me. But now You do, and I can't stand the thought that You not only know the truth, but You see the truth of who I am: a disappointment, a broken creation, an embarrassment." This defined my shame, this feeling of not wanting to be seen by the One who could solve it all. I understood why Adam and Eve hid, why they tried to cover themselves, and why they wanted to run from the very arms that could love them. It didn't make logical sense, but shame doesn't deal in the rational world, it lives and breathes in the fog of thought. I understood this dreadful word: *shame*.

I had carried that same shame with me for twenty years. An unknown man had taken me away. All this time I had believed he had only taken my physical innocence away, but now I knew he took a lot more. He said things to me that I carried as truth, just as Adam and Eve had carried Satan's lies as truth, and in believing what was spoken over me, I chose to believe the perspective of someone other than God. I chose to see myself through that man's eyes, through his lens, through his glasses, and I hadn't realized until now that I had kept his glasses on since then.

I heard from somewhere deep inside of me, *Take those glasses off and empty yourself. Empty yourself of those thoughts, feelings, and ideas of yourself. They aren't useful here. Empty them.*

What was hard about emptying myself of this shame was that I was so used to filling myself with it. I'd grown attached to shame, to this hatred for myself, because I'd carried it for so long. I kept feeding it and filling up with it. Shame had become such a part of me, I'd wrapped my identity around it. Out of fear, I hadn't told many people about my story. I didn't want to be told that it was, indeed, my fault and I deserved to be cast aside as dirty and broken. So I'd become an expert at diversions and distractions so no one knew the whole truth. My cover-ups were in my ambitions, my accomplishments, and my busyness. They were a constant fight to prove myself valuable and worthy of existence, yet, sadly, I had never felt like they had been enough.

If I stripped away my false self, I was left with a void. If I took away my shame, I lost my understanding of my identity. In both cases, I became a nothing. I owned nothing. I had no value. I didn't know what was worse for God to see: a soul clinging to some contrived sense of self or a soul wandering lifelessly. Emptiness is exactly as it sounds: vacant and void.

That is how I left the dumpster that day, feeling incredibly empty and vulnerable. I tried my hardest to leave shame in the green dumpster labelled 4—8180. As I started the engine of my van, I plastered a fake smile across my face to convince myself I could perform the rest of my day with my internal fuel gauge teetering close to empty. I hoped that there was enough drive inside of me to pour out my last drops of love onto my kids. As I drove away, I felt myself shift into autopilot. I felt hollow.

I arrived at the alley the fifth day, with a mixture of emotions I didn't know what to do with. I carried with me a little bit of scared, a touch of confusion, a smidge of tiredness, and a whole lot of irritation. I reluctantly sat down next to the dumpster, and my emotions rose up and out of me. *Why are You bringing me here? This is a ridiculous exercise, and I'm not finding any of the glorious visions of You. Instead, I'm being worn down and broken apart, and I'm questioning what any of this is accomplishing. I thought that this would bring me to a better understanding of Your love and care, but it has left me wondering how You've shown any love or care here. At least before this futile exercise, I was comfortable with how nice You felt while singing worship songs, while praying with other people, while experiencing Your love pour out on those around me. I was comfortable with feeling Your Spirit move in these kind places, and I was content with ignoring Your seeming indifference to my wound. It wasn't rejection, and that was a compromise I was willing to work with. Pushing off my wounds, my pain, my past seemed to be working, and I knew how to navigate that emotional landscape. I knew when to be happy, I knew when to suppress dark emotions, and I knew when to ignore the hurt that kept knocking at my heart's door. I knew how to do all of that. But now, You have taken all my strategies away and have exposed me.*

WEEK 1: GOD'S PRESENCE

At that moment, I was one of the Israelites who had wandered in the desert past the point of an adrenalin rush from escaping Egypt, past the point of excitement for a new adventure, and past the point of anticipation of all the promises God had laid out. I was an Israelite scoffing at how God's plan was unfulfilling, hard, and aimless. "Was it because there were no graves in Egypt that you brought us to the desert to die? What have you done to us by bringing us out of Egypt? Didn't we say to you in Egypt, 'Leave us alone; let us serve the Egyptians?' It would have been better for us to serve the Egyptians than to die in the desert!"[8] I was one of the Israelites begging for familiar territory and predictability. I was longing for the days where, even if they were hard, I understood how to navigate the pain to survive.

In college, one of my professors explained that even though it looked like Moses was called to take his people out of Egypt, his actual task was to take Egypt out of his people. The Israelites had grown up as slaves in Egyptian culture, and even though it was oppressive, they had been trained how to live there. Even though it meant certain death under the struggle and the pain, the certainty and predictability of that scene were, in a twisted way, safe. They knew the rules, they knew the consequences, they knew how to perform to get by. When Moses took the Israelites out of their familiar routine, they were scrambling for some bearings, some grounding, but they found none—which is why they were so quick to want to go back. This is the same reasoning why many abuse victims go back to living in disrespectful relationships: it's a familiar landscape to walk. It's why so many inmates become second and third-time offenders once they are let out of prison: it's a familiar culture. They haven't been given real-life tools to navigate such foreign territory.

This was where I stood. I was being called to leave a way of life I was used to and walk into uncharted territory for my soul. I was being asked to leave my Egypt behind and trust that my guide would provide for me in an entirely new landscape. I tried to look back, only to realize that God was holding out his hand and calling

8. Exod 14:11–12.

me forward. Going back wasn't an option anymore. But, honestly, I didn't like what I saw before me. Like the Israelites, all I saw was a raging sea that was most certainly going to be the death of me.

I started sitting at this dumpster on a Monday. The embarrassment of what I had been doing every morning while my kids attended a children's morning camp had stopped me from telling my best friend, my husband, what I had been doing all week long. It didn't feel like a Friday because I felt I had already walked for ages, and the soles of my shoes were about to wear out. However, when I saw that raging sea in front of me, I knew that I had to commit to the journey. This wasn't a challenge in jest anymore. This was no longer a quick test for God anymore. This was something I felt compelled to walk through. My soul needed it to survive.

So, I sat with my husband Nolan, and I explained to him this ludicrous idea that I was finding my way through pain into a place of healing by sitting at a dumpster for an hour every day. He hated the idea from the first time I told him. Every protective and defensive part of him wanted me to stop this crazy nonsense. But, he gave in, knowing that what was being moulded in my soul was something of the Spirit. That was something for which Nolan was willing to make concessions. I can't say it was easy for him to see his wife walk an unstable, rocky, and painful road. I prayed every day for God to bless him somehow through this because watching someone you love walk through a desert must be tough. Through it all, when he came home from his work, he held my hand, hugged my heart, and spoke words of encouragement and life to the deepest part of me. He believed in me, even when I didn't believe in myself.

The Saturday sun rose and brought early heat to the summer day. I kissed my husband goodbye and set out to sit in a filthy alleyway, while he enjoyed the luxury of sipping hot coffee to the sound of our kids playing video games in the basement.

Within ten minutes of leaving the house, I sat at the base of a dumpster, looking at the wheels of a parked storage trailer and listening to the sounds of forklifts loading and unloading merchandise into and out of their store. For six days, two wooden

## WEEK 1: GOD'S PRESENCE

skateboards had been propped up between the side of the building and the wheel of the trailer, but that morning, they were gone. My security radar sent out a quick S.O.S. into the air around me as I sensed the physical reality that I was not alone. Although I had come to know this spot as my sacred place, in reality, this was an obscure place where stolen things were stored and abandoned. Junk was salvaged and destroyed, and transients were welcomed and hated at the same time. I became a living part of this interplay, without realizing it; I was a part of the give-and-take of this back-alley culture.

Within this cycle of life, there was an allowance here to ask heretical questions. I wouldn't ask these questions that tormented my soul in a church, or a school, or a well-maintained house. My questions didn't make sense in those spaces. But in a back alley, it was as if nothing was impossible and all embarrassing and unconventional thoughts were able to seep out of me without even the slightest chastisement. I was testing those waters and dared to ask the great cloud of darkness, my most urgent questions.

*What were You thinking?*

The question escaped out of my brain, and I waited for the familiar desire to reel back in the thoughts I had cast out because they seemed wrong to ask. But, I had no desire to take it back. It felt good to set it free. So, I continued: *When You saw every demoralizing act that took place, what thoughts ran through Your mind? When You witnessed a girl stripped of all of her dignity and self-worth, what did You want to say to her?*

And there was a wonderful silence. If an answer came quickly, I would have thought it was a cover-up. If the answer was instantaneous, I would have thought God was giving me a quick answer because He didn't want to give me the *real* answer. But instead, there was contemplative silence which I cherished. My inner sceptic and malicious judge needed that wait time. He waited just long enough for the following words to well up inside of me:

*I can't answer that question with words yet. Your navigation point for understanding love was turned upside down that night. Your perception of comfort and affection was changed. I could become a hug, but you wouldn't accept it. I could be a voice, but you wouldn't converse with it. Any explanation I would give, you would discard as empty rhetoric. You would dismiss it as a language meant for another. Instead, I will let you experience my answer. Take time to live into my answer today, as I've been helping you live into my answer your whole life. And this is it. . . my answer is in my questions.*

*What do you suppose my mom was thinking while I hung on the cross?*

I thought about that. What was Mary thinking while she watched her son be tortured? While she watched her son go through hour after hour of agony? While she watched her son breathe his last breath while a mocking crowd surrounded him? I'm guessing the farthest from her mind were the judgemental, uncaring, and dismissive thoughts I accused Jesus of thinking of me. I pictured a heart breaking, a love unending, a mom wanting to take the pain and the abuse away. I pictured a woman that wanted to scream *"Stop!"* at the top of her lungs, to push away all the guards and the mockers and tell them to leave her son alone. I pictured a mom and a follower feeling every blow out of empathy for her son. Mary couldn't stop what was happening to Jesus, but she endured it with him.

*What do you suppose John, my best friend, was thinking while I hung on the cross?*

I thought about John. What was his best friend thinking? While Jesus bled in front of him, while his confidante sweat sorrow into the ground, when the man he had the deepest connection with hung limply on a cross in front of him, what was he thinking? I guessed scorn, ridicule, and abandonment wasn't his first response—the response I'd often thought an embarrassed Jesus thought of me. No, I pictured clenched fists that wanted to defend his friend, but knew it would be futile. I pictured a set jaw angry at the pain and wincing at the humiliation of his friend. I pictured a man who would have protective adrenaline pumping through his body, wanting to yell out in defence as the man on the other cross was mocking Jesus. I pictured a helpless man, feeling the anguish of his best friend. He couldn't stop the chain of events, but he was walking the road of pain as best as he could with his friend.

God was telling me that what Jesus' mom and his best friend felt towards Him was how He felt towards me. God wasn't helpless. God wasn't turning a blind eye in the depths of despair. He was, actually, the only one who stayed with me during that horrifying experience.

That night, during the rape, I learned to numb my thoughts. I learned how to become void of emotions. I learned to disassociate myself from feelings that threatened and attacked me. I'd carried that skill into a lot of situations in my life, but Jesus was breaking through that wall. The cross was lifted and fell into that hole in my heart, and Jesus' crucifixion became real and raw to me in all of its hideous vices: the humiliation, degradation, scorn, and shame. On the cross, Jesus spoke out what I have wanted to say for twenty years, "My God, my God, why have you forsaken me?"[9]

As a Red Bull can bumped its way on the concrete, carried clumsily by the wind, I came to the deep connection that Jesus had felt what I have felt. He endured pain, isolation, and abandonment as I had endured. He had been broken down just as I was. It was entirely different, but it was the same.

I know that what happened to me is my story. Just as every single human on this planet has their own tale of brokenness, hurt, pain, sorrow, and rejection. Everyone has an account of being seeped in shame—all different, yet all very real. There are no levels of shame. One act of hurt to one person connects them to the hurt of another. To those who have experienced abuse, depression, death, dementia, divorce, emotional isolation, mental illness, neglect, or PTSD. . . we all know shame. We are all in this together. Shame is an ocean where there are no comparisons, but there is a shared experience of being in over our head. We are all swimming and drowning and searching for a lifeboat.

Even Jesus. As He hung on the cross, even Jesus experienced the deep waters of shame. Only, He became the lifeboat which He called me to board. No discrimination, no regard to social

---

9. Matt 27:46.

importance or neglect. Come one, come all—broken, bruised, and lifeless—come aboard.

I felt something well up inside of me. A voice simply asking me to consider a new layer in my past. I was being asked to feel God's presence to the same measure as I felt the pain. It was such a new idea to me. The gospel I grew up with was one of replacement. Replace a bad experience with a good one. Replace a self-defeating thought with a self-affirming one. Replace a demon with an angel. It always sounded so simple, but it was an impossibility. How can you replace something key in shaping who you've become?

Jesus was providing the possibility of a path of endless life-giving choices. When Moses addressed the Israelites, after they were ready to listen and remember the promise of love towards them, he relayed this message from God: "See, I set before you today life and prosperity, death and destruction."[10] And then again, "This day I call heaven and earth as witnesses against you that I have set before you life and death, blessings and curses. Now choose life, so that you and your children may live and that you may love the Lord your God, listen to his voice, and hold fast to him. For the Lord is your life."[11] God wasn't replacing their past, in fact, he constantly reminded them of the pain of it. Instead, God was offering the choice to either live out the past again and again and perpetuate the damage or to choose life and live into His love over and over again and trust what might happen. Here, at a grimy dumpster, God was offering to me the same thing: live a life ruled by pain or live into one directed by a Holy Presence. I had always thought relief from this wound would be a one-time decision, like popular testimonies of the one moment that created a 180 turn-around in lives. But this wasn't anything like that. Thankfully, the offer would be constantly put on the table. *This day, this hour, this minute and again the minute after, choose life.* I've been asked to choose life while death is knocking at the door.

After my timer sounded, I left the dumpster that morning. I was unsure of this offer. I was unsure of what choosing life looked

---

10. Deut 30:15.
11. Deut 30:19–20a.

and felt like. It seemed like a blind step into a promising unknown. The inner pain I felt and carried and formed for so long seemed immense. Wrapping my head around the invitation to feel God's presence to the same measure of that pain seemed unlikely. I admit I didn't know a God who could be that big. Yet He had shown me that He was with me that evening twenty years ago, and the conversations that were welling up from inside of me let me know that His presence was real in this alley. There was no way I could create such conversations, and more so, there was no way I would have *wanted* to have such conversations. After one week into this experience, I was leaving a place where I thought God wasn't, and now I didn't want to leave because it was a place where God very much was.

# WEEK 2

## Shame

I RETURNED TO THE dumpster for a second week and sat down on the cement ledge that jutted out of the building. The dumpster and the adjacent rusty trailer were becoming familiar, almost comfortable to me. I had tucked myself up against the dumpster the previous week, scared of being seen, petrified of the possibility of being approached. That morning, I let my guard down a little and chose the ledge. To my left, I saw the traffic on the street speeding by, caught up in the hurry of a morning routine. Several people passed by, faces down, determined to reach their destination without interruption. To my right, I traced the stains of rust that seemed to have leaked from two metal knobs on the trailer down to the concrete. A puddle of copper colored metal seemed fused to the ground near my feet. I scuffed the ground, kicking up silt and dirt that settled on top of the discolored spot.

I took a deep breath and began the process of removing all of myself from within. My mind wanted to wander and roam the endless rabbit trails of thought. It wanted to jump around and explore all of the underdeveloped ideas, fragmented plans, and persistent worries. But, with determination, I was once again clearing space, sweeping the busyness of life out onto the porch, putting aside the day's to-do list and the reminders of all the chores that needed to be done. I needed to push out all of my clutter to make space for

## WEEK 2: SHAME

God's presence to surround me again. Finally, when my mind had nowhere to go, I sat and waited. The time passed by slowly, and my uncomfortable vulnerability surfaced again. The hatred for whom I had become inundated my thoughts, breaching the empty space I had desperately tried to create. Here I was, a grown woman sitting crumpled in an alley, unable to move forward any longer because I was so afraid of what the world would do if they knew how hurt I was. I was angry at myself because I knew that I shouldn't feel this way; intellectually I knew the gospel could set me free, but my heart was still trying to cover up the wounds of the hurt that kept bleeding out.

I still wanted an answer to my question. What is God thinking about when He sees me alone beside this dumpster? What was God thinking about when He saw what was happening to me back then? Throughout the last week, I was shown that I wasn't alone—I had experienced God's outer physical presence as well as an inner spiritual and emotional companion. He showed me the extent of His pain to let me know that He understood mine. The cross of shame became less of an event written in a book, and it became alive to me. The knowledge of His presence in a pain that was so deep became a gracious hand of empathy that extended towards me, but it seemed as if He was dodging my question: *What were You thinking about?*

Perhaps I could only pursue the question further because I had taken the time to mentally process the reality that Jesus, too, suffered tremendous pain. My emptied senses were filled with His presence, but my heart was still void before God. I was desperate for words, for sentences, for descriptions of who I was. I had tried so hard to take out all the descriptors I knew of myself—pathetic, worthless, unlovable, broken—and I had pushed them out waiting to hear if God would just place them right back in me. I waited for words of identity to be given to me.

I don't know why it came to my mind, but as I closed my eyes, I was reminded of a woman that was brought to Jesus to be condemned. The church leaders of the day brought her in and placed her before Jesus, while a bunch of them surrounded and watched:

> ... they said to Jesus, "Teacher, this woman was caught in the act of adultery. In the Law, Moses commanded us to stone such women. Now, what do you say?"
> ... But Jesus bent down and started to write on the ground with his finger. When they kept on questioning him, he straightened up and said to them, "If any one of you is without sin, let him be the first to throw a stone at her." Again, he stooped down and wrote on the ground."[1]

The story continues and shows how everyone dropped their stones and left the woman standing alone with Jesus still drawing in the sand.

Not only was it odd to suddenly remember this story, but more confusing to me was the fact that as I sat alone by the dumpster, I became that woman standing alone in the sand. Our sins were different, but our shame was the same. I hesitantly looked up and watched the backs of people walking away, and I looked down and saw Jesus, just doodling names in the sand beside me. I stood for five long minutes just stuck there, watching Jesus.

I wonder for how long Jesus stayed there. I wonder how many times the woman said thank you and in how many ways. "Thank you for saving me. Thank you for sticking up for me. Thank you for taking a stand for me. Thank you for speaking for me. Thank you for rationalizing for me. Thank you ... for staying here. Thank you for not leaving me." And I imagine Jesus just nodding his head, smiling, and carrying on with his sand doodles.

I sat down next to Jesus and started to trace my fingers in the sand too. I wondered if the woman said sheepishly, "You don't have to be here, you know." I wanted to know if she got to that uncomfortable silent stage where she just wanted to be alone because she was still aware of her past. I wanted to know because that was what I kept repeating to Him while I sat there. *Jesus, you can carry on now. You can move on to others more deserving. You don't have to sit here with me. I'm not worth your time. I'm a lost cause. I'm still broken. Just leave me here. I have nowhere to go.* For me to leave this spot and walk into town seemed daunting. People still knew who I

1. John 8:4–5, 6b–8.

## WEEK 2: SHAME

was. I still knew who I was. Maybe a stoning would have been better than walking around now with my past exposed.

I heard a whisper: *You need to put the stones down. I'm not leaving.* It was a soft voice, but firm. I didn't understand it until I looked down at the concrete by the dumpster and found that I wanted to pick up every rock that was embedded in the ground and hurl it at myself. Even though there was no one around to sentence me to the punishment I thought I deserved, all my thoughts towards myself were sharp stones in my hands. Stones of self-hatred, stones of fear, stones of mockery, stones of judgment. I had been throwing these stones at myself for years, forever slashing the wound of my past, making it impossible to heal. Jesus, still doodling in the sand, was telling me to put the stones down.

Honestly, I was having a really tough time obeying Jesus. These stones had explained my existence. They had been my explanation for all the pain, fear, hurt, and anger I had inside of me. Someone stole my innocence, a stranger who was there and now is gone, and I needed to point my finger of blame at someone. So, I'd been blaming myself all along. I must have caused that wound. I must have asked for the hurt. I must have enticed the offence. I must have done something, or else it wouldn't have happened! I was to blame, and for that, I must be condemned. As long as I gripped these stones in my hand, I couldn't believe any other storyline existed.

No matter what I told Jesus, no matter what story I spun, no matter how messy I made this situation, Jesus didn't seem interested in leaving me. He gave no indication of leaving this place beside me at the dumpster and in the sand. In the past, my pain caused people to withdraw from me. If they didn't leave, I usually ended up pushing them out. I didn't know how to embrace relationships with self-hatred by my side. In those times of solitude, I'd hurled the stones of condemnation at myself through self-harm. But with Jesus, I couldn't seem to find a way to divert the conversation. Jesus kept saying: *Just put the stones down. I'm not leaving.*

"Woman, where are they? Has no one condemned you?"
"No one, sir," she said.

"Then neither do I condemn you," Jesus declared. "Go now and leave your life of sin."[2]

If Jesus didn't condemn me, why did I? If Jesus was willing to leave the stones alone, why couldn't I?

I had spent so much time emptying my mind and my heart that I forgot to empty what was in my hands. I was beside Jesus, with God, Her Spirit surrounding me, and I couldn't even reach out and thank Him because my hands were full. If only I could put these stones down.

Paul writes in Romans, "There is now no condemnation for those who are in Christ Jesus because through Christ Jesus the law of the Spirit who gives life has set you free from the law of sin and death."[3]

The laws of the Old Testament made a lot of sense to me. They were all cause-and-effect; they were all about natural consequences. If you did something bad, you would be punished. If you had something that was broken, you threw it out. If something was unclean, you would isolate it until it had been deemed clean. But, somehow Jesus changed those rules. I don't fully know why, but he did. Motivated by love? Motivated my mercy? Motivated by grace? Motivated by something that is not of this world? The law of the Spirit gives life. If that Spirit was giving me life, a chance to live each day without condemnation for what has happened, what was stopping me? The offer was placed on the table once again: choose life or choose death.

I went home that day frustrated with myself because I couldn't make the most obvious, helpful, healing choice that was offered to me. It made no sense to me. Why couldn't I choose life over death? Why couldn't I choose to see freedom more than condemnation? Why couldn't I choose to experience presence more than isolation? Why couldn't I put down my stones?

Those questions kept running through my head that morning. I stepped through my front door and my kids leapt down the

2. John 8:10–11.
3. Rom 8:1–2.

## WEEK 2: SHAME

stairs to hug me. I gave them each a squeeze, but my mind was pre-occupied. As I folded laundry, cleared the counter of the dirty dishes, and went for a walk by the creek with my kids, my inability to choose life kept gnawing at me. I needed some help to sort through these thoughts. I needed guidance or my self-deprecating tendencies were going to overtake me. So, after I fed some lunch to my kids, I called up my pastor and arranged to meet that afternoon.

As I sat in his office, the news of what I was doing spilt out of me. From the decision to sit at a dumpster, to the reliving of my past, to the Biblical stories I was being drawn into, it all poured out of me. I expressed my disappointment with myself over the unanswered questions. I relayed my anxieties over facing Jesus and not knowing what to do. I explained how my heart was unwilling to surrender. My pastor listened. He was gracious. He gave space for the emotions and encouraged the struggle. He didn't give pat answers, nor did he try to suppress the unorthodox questions. Instead, he offered insight and avenues of thought to pursue. I knew then, that I needed to keep meeting with him to help ground the experiences I was having. I needed help and accountability in determining if these ruminations were theologically sound or if they were irrational thoughts from a thirsty and worn out desert traveller. So, we agreed to meet every couple of weeks.

The next day, I left my kids to watch tv while I went to the alley and tackled the glaring question as to why I was unable or unwilling to put my stones of condemnation down and choose the life that God was offering me. It didn't take much time at all for the answer to become so crystal clear to me: I wasn't putting the stones down because I thought the stones gave me control. When I was convinced that God was taking a leave of absence in my life, I took on the responsibility of running my own universe. I trusted my judgment more than God's. I trusted my plan more than His. I believed that I knew how to solve my problem and God could just watch and check in once in a while and be proud of my efforts. I hadn't considered that it was ok to stumble and fall on this path of life. I hadn't thought it was ok to be in need while wandering in this desert. I wasn't willing to accept that I was imperfect, that I was allowed to fail, that I was allowed to have questions and doubts. I was equipped with these stones in my hand to hurl at all my insufficiencies.

I had such high expectations of myself, and I couldn't handle the out-of-control me. Jesus was asking me to simply trust Him, not in part, but in whole. Jesus was holding out his hand, ready to take the stones away from me if only I would surrender my pride, if only I would accept that I wasn't in control and I was still going to be ok. I had to face the reality that the stones I held were doing me no good. My control was not very effective. I had to face the truth that I was an awkward, fallible, imperfect person who didn't have life figured out and never would. I wasn't being asked to let go of mere stones; I was being asked to let go of my kingdom, my vain thought that I could be in control like God. Gently and softly, Jesus was drawing pictures in the sand of my hands dropping stones and walking into a kingdom ruled by grace and mercy.

In the quiet, save for the crow that kept cawing above my head, I approached this idea of self-acceptance timidly. In the silence, my "poor in spirit"[4] self stood so plainly out in the cold, waiting for someone to love her as she was. She was so calm and patient, and I wondered why I was so reluctant to accept her.

But then I did. I brought her into the warmth of my heart because I saw that love was her only hope. I realized that the only way she would be able to survive was if I accepted her without condition. I looked upon her as if she were my own child and loved her as such.

And then the offer was once again thrown on the table: choose life or choose death.

Since it seemed like I was in a mood for accepting things, I chose life. I handed over the keys to my poorly built kingdom that had been under attack for years, and I very slowly walked through the open gates of God's love. I didn't even know what the place would be like or what it would bring, but I chose it anyway. In doing so, I felt a couple of the stones slip through my fingers, and I heard them hit the ground.

4. Matt 5:3.

Ironically, when I finally chose life, a blanket of darkness enveloped me. I felt it wrap itself around me until it was inside, above, beside, and behind me. I was in a darkness that was surprisingly familiar and comforting. It was like a weighted blanket, holding me still and absorbing the trembling fear that coursed through my body.

When I was a very young girl, I remember many times of feeling overwhelming sadness. I remember crying in my bedroom for all the broken parts of the world. I was overwhelmed by the pain and the hurt of all the creatures of the earth. How did I know their hurt? I don't fully comprehend, but at times I've just felt the loss of hopes, the loss of dreams, the loss of goodness as evil seemed to overtake. I have vivid memories of my dad shaking his head as if this was just a faze. I can clearly see my mom's face of concern as she watched me stew over problems that were the world's and not mine. And yet, I remember going to bed at night, and as I would turn off the light, I would feel the darkness fill up the room around me. I liked that feeling. It was as if it was insulation from the hurt turning to harm. God was in the dark of the night.

When I was a bit older, maybe grade three, I often took all my bedding and slept on my closet floor. It was darker there, it was more confined there, it seemed safer there. God felt closer there. In junior high, I loved going out to lay on our freshly cut lawn (the best smell in the entire world). I would stare up at the darkened sky, and I would try my hardest to see into the depths of darkness. It brought up pure wonder and amazement, and also, I gained a sense of comfort knowing that the thickness of darkness that surrounded me was the same dark particles that held the stars and moon in its place. When I was in college, as a physics major, I had the opportunity to study dark matter—the concept that there is something in the nothing we see. Dark matter proves, through mysterious gravitational pulls and light bending, that in the darkness, a Something exists. It dawned on me that a lot of my life has been uncovering the Somethings in what I thought were Nothings.

I remember, also during my college years, walking through the Stations of the Cross and watching Jesus carry and falter over the sins of this world. The depth of sadness that was brought to the cross often would overtake and overwhelm me. But then, the same blanket of darkness overcame me and astonished me. Sometimes I encounter God in the lightest and brightest and joyous places. But it would be a tragedy for me not to acknowledge His soothing presence in the dark when I am alone and can't even see the place where I need to step next. Those are the places that, for me, heartache and heaven collide.

Somewhere in the darkness, I heard an alarm sound. I got up from my filthy seat wondering if I could take the dark blanket with me. I wanted this mystery that linked arms with surrender to follow me. As I walked across the loading zone to my van, I slowly adjusted my eyes to the lights of the world and felt the shadow drape behind me like a superhero's cape. I was relieved to know I had the invincibility of the Spirit with me as I continued to process what self-acceptance and life looked like in my daily routine.

Getting to the dumpster the next day was impossible. I drove up to the parking stall and as I reached out to open my door, I was paralyzed by fear. I looked around at what had been such a quiet and solitary space and saw people walking around that I had not seen before. One lady hastily pulled a shopping cart of garbage and bottles behind her. One man kept popping out from a loading zone across the parking lot incessantly scratching himself. I was used to a rough-looking couple sitting by the back doors of another store smoking cigarettes, having their Tim Horton's coffee, and chatting in the early mornings. The skinny man always wore his green vest, and the woman alternated between a black top and a blue one. Today she wore her black one. But that morning, there were two more gruff men by them, talking violently with their hands. Their curse words and colorful language bounced off the building walls and penetrated the shell of my van.

Usually, a couple of delivery trucks would back up into their loading zones and, after a while, drive away while I sat in my place. Today, however, trucks were everywhere, their brakes making hissing noises, their wheels squealing, their doors banging, their

## WEEK 2: SHAME

chains scraping along the ground. I was jumping in my seat at every sound.

I couldn't bring myself to open the door. My trembling hand just couldn't do it. Panic rose in me, and I was incapacitated. Every rational fear surfaced along with every irrational one. What would I do if one of the gruff men approached me? What would I do if the hand-talkers touched me? What would I do if a delivery truck turned too wide and his trailer started backing up into me? What if I was pinned behind the trucks, forcing me to cry out and draw attention to myself. What if? What if?

I stayed in the safety of my van that day, and the tears came from my eyes. Slowly at first, and then like a flood they poured out from my body. I bawled big huge tears that drenched my shirt as they rolled down my cheek. I was shaking badly, and I could hear my heart racing with an irregular pattern in my eardrums. My neck felt hot, my ears were on fire, and I continued to cry because as much as I wanted to get out of the van, fear pushed up against my lungs and my heart. I think I was having a panic attack. Tears rolled down my cheek for the entire hour, unceasing, continual tears that ran from a seemingly endless supply from somewhere inside of me. I cried out my fear; I cried out my pain; I cried out my self-reliance. I drove home at the end of the hour with no more tears to give. I had run dry.

Making soul transforming decisions while wandering in my desert was hard. I chose life, freedom, and God's full presence while wandering in a wilderness of all places. The psalms are full of these decisions and calling out to God to listen and hear and be near. They speak of deer that are satisfied with the stream's water. There are songs of trees with roots reaching deep and the branches growing strong; there are poems that show the stars and moon and point out to God's providence. But there didn't seem to be any streams, or trees, or stars or moons in my desert. My landscape was one of garbage, cigarette butts, peeling paint, cracked cement, rusted metal, urine stains and dumped out coffee puddles. Choosing life here was ironic. God showing up here was even more surprising. The courage to keep walking the desert was still a struggle, but I knew there was only one way out: through to the other side. I suspected that if I did walk out of this dumpster landscape, I would find myself in a new place, where I would have to make a life-and-death decision again. Perhaps that is what Jesus meant when He said: "Whoever wants to be my disciple must deny themselves and take up their cross *daily* and follow me."[5] This, I decided, would be a lifelong task: to continually remind myself to deny my control every day, pick up the brokenness I feel all the time and skip on after Christ to find out what he has in mind for me to do today.

I managed to get out of my van the following day and found my place between the garbage and the trailer. I was afraid that my feelings of panic and fear would overtake me, but I was relieved to see the loading zones and the parking lot vacant. I was, once again, alone. While staring at the paint that was peeling off of the green dumpster, I asked Jesus: *How is it possible for you to see the beauty in brokenness?*

My mind wandered to the stained-glass windows that circled and enclosed the churches of my early 20's. I loved how the colors seemed to come to life when the natural light of the sun shone through. I remembered my fascination with the images just beyond the window and how they would change depending on what color I was looking through. The tree leaves could be a lush green, a fiery orange, or a gloomy blue all at the same time depending on which window I peered through. As I sat in the grey tones of the alley, I realized that I'd been looking at myself and the world through stained windows. We all have—through stains of hurt, stains of love, stains of anger, stains of joy, stains of sadness, and stains of peace. Understanding ourselves or the events around us isn't so much about what we are looking at, but finding out what colored pane we choose to look through. So, how does Jesus see beauty in brokenness? Perhaps He found the windowpane that I have struggled to find. The one that reveals the goodness, the peace, the wonder of the world as it was created to be. My mind tries to convince me that He looks through a pure and untouched window, but I don't think that's the case. Maybe the best perspective is standing

5. Luke 9:23.

## WEEK 2: SHAME

beside Jesus and peering through His blood-stained window of the cross. Perhaps the windowpane that I think is discoloured by murder, shame, death and humiliation is a lens that reveals creation as worthy, beautiful, and redeemed.

It was the last day of my second week at the dumpster, and I found myself back with Jesus sitting in the sand. As I pushed the granules of sand around, I pushed all of my thoughts out of my mind and tried to focus solely on Jesus. I was getting more efficient at this exercise, but it still took so much energy. I still liked to be the one in charge of my thoughts. I liked to direct where my mind wandered. But, that's not what this experience was about. This was about waiting on God. I was gradually learning to trust His stirring and His movements in this place.

When all was clear, and it was just the sound of breathing, Jesus looked at me suddenly and with wide eyes, He asked me: *Have you met my dad?* He asked it as if He were a little boy. He asked it with innocence and wonder. He asked it with excitement, with anticipation, with genuine adoration and pride for who his dad was.

In contrast, I took offence to the question. Have I met his dad? Have I met God? Of course I have! I recalled meaningful times of prayer, study, worship, contemplation, fasting and celebration. I remembered how He responded, answered, guided and helped. I thought back to the times that I felt alive, fueled by a mysteriously wonderful Spirit, and felt a wholeness and a peace in depths of my soul. How could I explain all of those experiences though?

The thoughts that jumbled around in my head were hedged in by annoyance and disbelief that Jesus would ask this question. But when I looked up, I saw that Jesus didn't want an answer, or a defence, or an explanation. He just really wanted me to meet his dad, whether for the first time, the thirteenth time, or the seventy-seventh time. A little wave of relief washed over me, as I realized that I hadn't been put on the spot. Throughout His life, Jesus continually asked people this question, so I shouldn't have been surprised. He was always pointing out His Father to those around him.

I responded as relevant to our situation at the dumpster as I could. *Yeah, He was in the shadows of the alley that night.* I tried to suppress that feeling of shame that was knocking at my heart. I refused to open the door. Then Jesus responded in a peculiar way: *Oh, Dad's in the dark. I was the one in the shadows.* I scoffed inwardly. As if there were a distinction between the two.

How could the dark be different than the shadow? Again, I was brought to that dreadful night. I sat in the aftermath on the pavement by the dumpster. I was alone as I watched the stranger run in the other direction. It felt dark all around me. Then I looked to the direction I saw God the first time, standing in the dark shadows. I looked at the place where I sensed His presence. When I looked, I saw a foot take a step forward. Out Jesus emerged. I tried to divert my attention, but I couldn't stop. Jesus stood in front of me bearing the evidence of my wounds. His hair was matted, his face scuffed, his shirt was stretched out, and his pants were stained and torn. I closed my eyes, but still saw the blood and bruises. His hands were trembling with mine. Jesus was right. He was the one in the shadows. He didn't just know suffering—he knew *my* suffering. He bore *my* wounds, He bore *my* shame, He bore *my* insufficiencies. He bore it all.

God was indeed in the dark. God was everywhere and all around me. My world went unexplainably dark that night, and God was in that darkness. I think I knew that all along; I just didn't know I was allowed to embrace that aspect of my faith among fellow believers. I didn't know that I could choose life by choosing the dark. Barbara Brown Taylor, an author who dared to explore the topic of spiritual darkness, wrote,

> For those who have suffered from this division of their days, doing their best to stay on lit paths and avoid dark places without ever quite shaking the sense that they are shutting themselves off from something vital for their souls, there is another way. There is a whole dark night of spiritual treasure to explore.[6]

---

6. Taylor, *Learning to Walk*, 172.

## WEEK 2: SHAME

I think I finally allowed myself to see the darkness as good, even helpful. Wrapping myself under its covers and hugging Her presence around me tightly, I drove home to be with my family. I exhaled with relief as I parked in my driveway. It was as if I had been given permission to experience God in *all* of the places of my life, but even more thrilling was the fact that God took me up on my original challenge. Was He willing to step into the difficult places of life? Yes, in fact, He was waiting for me there the whole time.

"Have mercy on me, my God, have mercy on me, for in you I take refuge. I will take refuge in the shadow[darkness] of your wings until the disaster has passed."[7]

---

7. Ps 57:1.

# WEEK 3

# Healing

When Moses went up Mount Sinai to commune with God, he spent forty days there. The book of Exodus explains that a cloud covered the mountain while the presence of God settled on it, and Moses "entered the cloud as he went up the mountain. And he stayed on the mountain forty days and forty nights."[1] Two things strike me as I read this passage. First, Moses willingly walked into the darkest and scariest of all places. Earlier in Exodus, it describes how Mount Sinai trembled violently and earthquakes kept shaking the place. To the Israelites, it looked like a consuming fire was at the top of the mountain and smoke kept billowing out of the top. Then, that same thick smoke settled in and around the mountain leaving it dark and foreboding. This was a place that no one wanted to or even dared to enter. Until Moses. Moses entered the cloud on his own accord. As scary as it was to enter into the dark presence of God, Moses knew he had to. He was summoned there. It was his way to meet, speak, and receive from God.

I came back to the dumpster, a place where my memories were being covered in the cloud of God's presence. My understanding of my past was being choked out from the billows of smoke while a new vision was taking its first breaths. My heart

---

1. Exod 24:18.

was trembling violently, but my soul was being reformed. Almost every night, I had sat on the back porch with my husband, debriefing the days. Through my stories and ramblings that didn't make sense when they were just blurted out, Nolan knew of the refining process I was going through. He was scared for my safety, physical and emotional, but he also understood the necessity to continue. He trusted, that if God had taken me this far, that He would guide me through. I, too, knew I was alone in the dark safety of a fierce God that was smelting my soul.

Secondly, I am struck by how long Moses was gone. It's not so much the length of time I'm concerned about, but *how* he passed that much time within those forty days. I highly doubt that God was talking his ear off every single second. I'm sure God allowed time for sleeping, for finding comfortable places to rest, for finding new winding roads to walk on the rugged terrain. Although the material Moses came away with from Mount Sinai was extensive, laying out commandments and the directives for the tabernacle, I doubt that the entire time was a rigorous seminar. I think there was a space given to rest in God's dark presence, filling Moses up with what he needed through the healing sounds of silence. I hope that it was in the quiet that he found confidence in God, peace with what he was called to do, and an assurance that God would stay with him regardless of what he might find when he left the mountain.

I spent the Monday of the next week in silence. Even the traffic on the street seemed to be lighter, the loading zones had fewer deliveries and the regular parking lot wanderers seemed to tip-toe past me. Someone must have cleaned the channel between the trailer and the brick wall over the weekend because the disposable coffee cup that usually rolled back and forth near the back wheel was missing. The sounds that echoed from when it bumped and bounced on the pavement were gone. I could have come to many conclusions about that silence. I could have thought God was snubbing me, that He stood me up, that He had better things to do than to interact with me. I think the "me" from two weeks ago would have jumped to those conclusions, but that wasn't my assumption this time. Jesus whispered to me as if I was one of His disciples, "*Come with me by yourself to a quiet place and get some rest.*"[2] I sat in glorious silence for an hour, immersed in His presence, comforted by being in the shadow of His wing. No thoughts or scenes or pictures entered my mind, forcing me to process ideas and events I felt too tired to go through. I was given rest and assurance that I was still held by Him in the quiet.

The next day, resting was not an option. I was restless as I sat, tapping my foot against the side of the green dumpster and scratching at the rip that was forming in my jeans. But my mind couldn't focus on the world around me as I was taken into a world where Jesus and I were walking along a dusty road. I stared down at the path, billows of dusty dirt rose with every step I took. I was having trouble with the duplicity (triplicity? Is that even a word?) of the nature of God the Father, God the Son, and God her Holy Spirit. I knew them and interacted with them separately on this journey, yet it was as if Jesus would dissipate if God's presence was gone. It was as if the Holy Spirit's breath in me would be sucked dry if Jesus stopped walking with me. They couldn't exist separately even though I met them as such. In this confusion, I asked Jesus: *Where is God?* I asked it out of innocence, not defiance. I just wanted His cloud before us or His pillar of fire to show us direction. I knew God was with us, but somehow not. Like the well-intentioned teenager listening to the teacher, but thinking about something entirely different. Present, but not there. Jesus responded by stating quite simply, *Oh, He's tending to our wounds.*

My heart skipped in an irregular beat at that. Was I more taken aback by the word *tend* or the word *our*? I couldn't choose. I thought I'd dissect the latter first.

What was He meaning with this "our wounds" business? My mind flashed back to the memory of Jesus stepping out of the shadows. I didn't like that picture, but I couldn't erase it from my mind. First of all, I didn't like it because, quite simply, I didn't enjoy seeing pain. Secondly, and more importantly, it meant that Jesus felt *my* pain specifically. I grew up with the universal truth that

---

2. Mark 6:31.

## WEEK 3: HEALING

Jesus suffered on the cross and died for the sins of the *world*. That always seemed generic and, well, nicely packaged in vague terms. All sins, all hurt, all suffering, all pain were collectively felt by Jesus. But that image brought on an uncomfortable intimacy with Jesus and my specific wounds. He made them *our* wounds. This truth crossed the line from universal into unified, public into personal. A lump formed in my throat—not out of shame anymore, but out of a foreign feeling of being completely known by someone. I stole a glance over to Jesus and discovered that he was still covered in the scuffs and the evidence of my pain.

While he bore my wounds, Jesus was still willing to walk beside me.

Then, I turned to the word "tend." Within that word, there was another layer of commitment. To tend implies long-term care. When someone tends to a wound, they don't slap a bandage on it and call it good. They don't rinse away the dirt and send the person on their way. When someone tends to a wound, they patiently take the time to care. Wounds need to be wrapped up, then unwrapped, cleaned, and wrapped again. All this work is put in to stave off infection, prevent permanent damage, and to prevent the loss of function of the area. Unfortunately, my wounds seemed to have done all three. The infection of fear and self-hatred had seemed to overtake me. The damage was twenty years fresh and felt unalterable, and I was afraid that I might have lost the function of trust in my heart. It felt overwhelming. God had a lot to attend to. Yet, Jesus said He was busy *tending our wounds*.

Healing, as much as I want it to be instantaneous, involves wait time and gradual miracles. I wonder if He made it a process so I wouldn't forget his character through it all. A quick healing could have made me misinterpret God's work in my life as a pop in/pop out magician. A hasty healing could have made me think God gave me a couple of minutes to address my needs and then moved on. An instantaneous healing might have led me to lean on carefully crafted prayers for results rather than God Himself. At worst, a healing through someone might have accidentally made me put my faith in that person rather than the God of all life. Any gift that

I received from God, including healing, needed to bring me closer to the gift giver. Tending, nursing wounds, checking on progress and reworking the regiment needed for complete care was God's way for me to lean on Him and learn of His character.

When Lazarus was sick, Mary and Martha called up Jesus and asked for a favor. "Make him better," they asked. "Heal him like you heal others," they pleaded. "Will you help?" they inquired. "Your good friend is dying." When Jesus heard "that Lazarus was ill, he stayed two days longer in the place where he was."[3] What? Jesus seemed so aloof, so distant, so harsh. And yet, was He in the process of tending? Of preparing and repairing? Was he giving due time to bring the healing when it would confirm who God was in the middle of pain? Was time the unexpected gift for Mary and Martha so they could truly recognize and accept the magnitude of care God was showing them? After four days of being broken by death, Lazarus became unbroken, and new life emerged.

There was an army commander called Naaman in the book of 2 Kings. He was prestigious, successful, and valiant . . . and he had a skin disease, probably leprosy. In historical terms, he was a dead man walking. Time would be his nemesis, and eventually, his body would be overtaken so much that his role and his identity would be taken from him. He went to the great prophet Elisha to receive healing and left the interchange pouting and angry that he didn't get healed right away. "'I thought that he would surely come out to me and stand and call the name of the Lord his God, wave his hand over the spot and cure me of my leprosy'. . . so he turned and went off in a rage."[4] Instead of instantaneous healing, Naaman was told to go to the muddy Jordan and wash himself not once, but seven times, to become clean. These instructions were annoyingly tedious and kind of gross. There are other rivers cleaner than the swampy Jordan. And, seven times? Don't you think that is a little excessive? Was this a process of trust? Was this God tending to his wounds? Preparing and repairing the damage? Was He giving due time to bring the healing that would make it look less like a magic

---

3. John 11:6.
4. 2 Kgs 5:11, 12.

act and more like a divine one? Was the time it would take to go to the Jordan and wash seven times a gift for Naaman to truly recognize and accept a God that cared about him, even in the muddy places? With no other options to take, Naaman went to the Jordan River and washed up seven times. Naaman went back to Elisha and said, "'Now I know that there is no God in all the world except in Israel.'"[5] After years of being broken down by a death sentence, Naaman became unbroken, and new life emerged.

By caring for me day in and day out, I was learning how to lean on and learn of God's love, joy, peace, patience, kindness, goodness, faithfulness, gentleness, and self-control.[6] In tending to my wounds, God was feeding me His fruit, fruit I often overlooked along the way. I had seen glimpses here and there. I mean, I haven't led a completely ungrateful life. But I don't know if I saw my small miracles as events connected to my life's healing process. I didn't realize that each unbroken part of me that I found along the path of my life was all to show the magnitude of God's care. It was to show how He was, and is, and always will be in the business of calling up new life from all the places in my life that have died a good death, but need to live again in His strength.

For instance, it's a small miracle that I didn't die completely that horrible night. That I had enough physical fight in me to make it stop in enough time to give me the strength to find my way out of the alley. It seemed surreal, but it was, in fact, real. I was able to get out of the alley, make it to a nearby restaurant, wash up (which I did out of impulse and didn't realize I was washing away the evidence police needed), call for help, willingly get in the confines of a car, go through police reports, and eventually make it home. All of those things I did in the aftermath were impossible, and therefore must be a miracle from God, because I wasn't able to do much of anything for the next couple weeks. Getting out of my bed every morning after was one of the most difficult things to accomplish.

It's also a small miracle that later I completed college. Anyone who knows me would be confused by that statement because I love

5. 2 Kgs 5:15.
6. Gal 5:22, 23.

learning. I love discovering, dissecting, unearthing, contemplating, connecting, and building. I feel most alive when my brain is buzzing. But the true miracle is in the logistics of college. I triple majored in Physics, General Science, and Theology which are academic streams that are not known for their overwhelming female populace. The fact is, I had to walk into classes every day full of college guys and sit beside them, complete labs with them, spend long nights together working through theorems and calculus problems, work through Calvin's Institutes with them, while the entire time I was afraid of them—some slightly more than others. But I did it. I became a little more unbroken, and new life was starting to emerge.

Four years after I was raped, I was a speaker at a church retreat, and I met a very kind and sweet guy. He didn't scare me or frighten me; he intrigued me. This was a foreign feeling for me, so I did what any enamored girl would do: avoid him completely and become friends with his sister. A year later, out of that friendship and pure superhuman power, I summoned enough strength to ask him if he would like to go out for dinner with me. I glanced in the mirror at that new unbroken part of me and proceeded to date, fall in love, and marry that sweet man. I make it sound like it was easy, but that would not represent that time well at all. There were lots of dates that ended in handshakes, many awkward social exchanges, streams of tears that were sorting out my worthiness of love or affection, kisses that were wanted but never taken, and hugs that took time to iron out the stiffness of my body. I didn't think I would ever be able to love, but God tended to that wound carefully—as if he had healing through this particular man planned out for me from before time began.

One of my biggest fears was that due to the damage a stranger caused me I might not be able to have kids. After I was raped, and the police found out I had already washed myself, I was too embarrassed to go to a doctor to see how badly I was hurt. Plus, that would mean I'd have to tell my parents everything that happened—something I hadn't done. I was a vault, and I hid the key. I fled, avoided, and ran from any appointment that would make

## WEEK 3: HEALING

me face the internal results of the night. However, as my wedding day approached, I didn't know if I could marry the good man God had given me if I wasn't able to have his kids. God must have been carrying that fear, that hurt, that wound so tenderly and worked at those bandages fervently for six years. A couple of months before my wedding date, I reluctantly went to see my doctor so she could assess the damage. The news I received confirmed that God had never left my side and was healing me in the long term because I was told that, although there was excessive scar tissue, there wasn't enough damage to stop me from becoming pregnant. My husband and I have three wonderful miracles that I carried and gave birth to, each of whom proves that God has always been in the business of taking broken things and making them unbroken, giving the chance for new life to emerge.

Had everything been healed and fixed up the day after that cold January night, I don't know if I would have understood the magnitude of God's care for me. Emptied here in this alley, all the years of healing culminated into an awareness of the Spirit's touch and Her constant presence in my life. St. John of the Cross once wrote, "In the inner stillness where meditation leads, the Spirit secretly anoints the soul and heals our deepest wounds."[7] In the silence here, I was being let in on the secret. My thoughts turned to Jesus and His death on the cross. Jesus had to die and stay that way for three days to ensure He was really dead according to Jewish custom. He needed to wait the agonizing three days before He could resurrect, before brokenness became unbroken for good. It was and is His long-term plan, the secret anointing on our souls, that through all the years of hurt and pain that takes place between that Friday and Sunday, God is in the habit of tending wounds.

When I arrived at the dumpster the next couple of days, I sat as if I were admitted to the in-patient care program. I was well into this spiritual journey, a treatment of sorts, but my body was having a hard time accepting all that was good for healing. One day I was sitting listlessly in the summer's heat and the monotony

---

7. Contemplative Monk (@Contemplative Monk), *St. John of the Cross*, Facebook, July 23, 2019.

of the alley, the next I nearly fell asleep as I was curled up on the ground next to snuffed out cigarette butts. I was there, but could hardly account for what happened during the single hour of each day. Time seemed to get blurry: the seconds ticked away slowly and then suddenly went feverishly fast. I knew that I had let go of fragments of my old self, but I was sinking in discouragement because I didn't know how to proceed forward. I didn't know what questions to ask, what thoughts to ponder, what direction to consider. Richard Rohr, an author and Franciscan friar whose writings I respect and resonate with, writes about the headspace I was in during those couple of days at the dumpster.

> Liminal Space comes from Liminia, which is the Latin word for threshold, the space betwixt and between. Liminal space, therefore, is a unique spiritual position where human beings hate to be but where the biblical God is always leading them. It is when you have left the "tried and true" but have not yet been able to replace it with anything else. It is when you are finally out of the way. It is when you are in between your old comfort zone and any possible new answer. It is no fun . . . Think of Israel in the desert, Joseph in the pit, Jonah in the belly. . . If you are not trained in how to hold anxiety, how to live with ambiguity, how to entrust and wait—you will run—or more likely you will "explain."[8]

I was on a threshold, not having the energy to run nor the mental capacity to sort any of my thoughts. I sat in the space between progress and regression, joy and sadness, peace and restlessness, hope and despair. My emptiness was quickly becoming my nemesis as I sank into apathy. I was stuck in the in-between, and in this liminal space, I didn't even care.

I have a friend who is, to put it in blunt terms, obsessed with Enneagram tests and results. The personality test has helped her sort out her thoughts, responses, and actions. Not only that, but it has helped her to relate to others by knowing how words dance around in people's minds differently, how thoughts can be trapped

---

8. Rohr, "Grieving as Sacred Space," para. 4.

## WEEK 3: HEALING

in some but roam too freely in others, and how actions and reactions have various output rates depending on the tendencies of one's personality. She encouraged me to take this test as a possible window to view the 'stuckness' I found myself in. As sceptical as I was (a true five with a four-wing on the Enneagram scale would know), I took the test and in one of the explanations I found a peculiar word that shone a spotlight on much of my life.

*Melancholy*. The Lexico online dictionary defines it as a "pensive sadness."[9] The Enneagram descriptors say that at times I can feel "depleted, drained of sufficient resources and life force"[10] Digging further into this concept, I discovered a better word to describe many periods of my life. Kathleen Norris, a poet and essayist, describes the ancient word, *acedia*. She explains,

> The Greek word acedia just means not caring. It's come to mean as seriously not caring to the extent that you no longer care that you care. I described it as a spiritual morphing. If you really give in to it, it becomes this numbing effect on your life. Just knowing the name of what it is, it's not depression, it's not just sadness. It's not boredom and restlessness, but all those things are a part of it... Depression is an illness, whereas acedia is a temptation.[11]

Acedia is apathy in the heart and soul of a person. It's where the will to fight on and fight through is non-existent. It is often described in reference to monks who devoted their lives to routine and monotonous living. Author and theologian, Jerry Sittser, describes how acedia is best translated as "impatience with routine... a desire for a shortcut—that's what it really implies. That's why they call it the noonday demon. But the time noon hits when you're living in a monastery and you've prayed for the fourth or fifth time of the day, you look outside and the sun has basically stopped moving."[12]

In reading over journals from the past, I've noticed this theme runs strong. Whether I'm proud of it or not, this tendency

---

9. Lexico.com, s.v. "melancholy."
10. "Enneagram Theory."
11. Norris, "Fighting the Noonday Demon," para. 57,60.
12. Norris, "Fighting the Noonday Demon," para. 63.

towards thoughts on the futility of life has been a part of me since I was little. I remember journaling over and over, "What is the point of this all?" or "What am I striving to become?" or "How does my life matter in the whole of everything?" I always felt a kindred spirit with the author of Ecclesiastes who yelled out into a world that didn't want to listen, "Utterly meaningless! Everything is meaningless!"[13]

There is a fine line I walk, however, between glorifying and hating this part of me. I glorify it in a way because I've come to love this part of me. It drives me to ask big questions; it pushes me to think deeper about the everyday affairs of life and spirituality. Through these melancholic times, I've learned to live more intentionally, love more deeply, and develop grit in my passion to make something of this life God breathed into me. However, when I don't find acceptable answers to my questions, I am thrown into a dark pit of despair that is difficult to climb out of. My problem is that I often don't realize I've fallen in until I've hit the bottom.

Throughout those couple of days, I found myself restless with this daily routine. I knew I had accomplished so much, yet my mind wasn't registering the distance I had travelled. It was as if I was in the middle of crossing the Red Sea and couldn't even see the water that had parted for me. I looked back, and all I saw was my self-created demons gaining ground on me. I looked forward, and I couldn't make out the other shore. The monotony here was killing me. The seconds ticked by with nothing to show for it.

I met with my pastor that afternoon. I explained how I felt I had taken two steps forward, but three steps back. I tried to make sense of my depressive thoughts and my desire to give up, but the words came out jumbled and mixed up. My hands were shaking and tears were threatening to pour out. I felt ungrateful for the work God was doing and embarrassed that I wasn't able to focus on progress. Again, my pastor simply sat with me in my sadness. His encouragement came in the form of validating the reality of my thoughts while gently pointing out that progress, no matter how big or small, is still progress. The mere step of sitting near the

13. Eccl 1:2.

## WEEK 3: HEALING

dumpster was a way of pushing forward, he pointed out. So, with a shaky heart, I resolved to sit in the dreary and repetitive alley yet again the following morning.

If I was looking for change, I got it the next day. As I walked up to my usual spot, a wave of offended anger rose in me. The wall and the trailer that I stared at were tagged. Bright blue spray paint covered the area in nonsense thug-wanna-be jargon. I was so angry because it was an intrusion into my space. This was my home. I had hated this place at first, but now I had grown attached to it because I could be myself here. This place had become my sanctuary, my confessional, the holy doors leading to the altar where I was meeting God. It was my church, my tent of meeting. And someone had desecrated it.

My anger melted slowly into amused contemplation. After all, it was just spray paint in an alley. Most people would say such an act is a given here. It fits in with the garbage on the ground, the wasps feeding on the dumpster's contents, and the overall grey-tones of the scene. But the spray paint made me chuckle—eventually. It was such a little change to this place, like changing the lampshade in a living room. It was just enough newness to help me recognize what a little change can do to a place. Just when I thought this place was leading me down the familiar path of despair and futility, all along it had been slowly bringing small changes to my interior landscape. Things were being tagged and rearranged inside without my full consent, bringing an unforeseen newness to places I thought were stale.

Our culture likes to celebrate and announce change loudly. Shout-it-from-the-rooftops with a megaphone style: social media posts going viral, YouTube channels shared and overshared, full-page ads in newspapers, a famed spot on the six o'clock news. People like the dramatic and are drawn to sensationalism. Quiet change, slow change, is often overlooked or diminished in its meaning. The world rarely honors the snail-like narrative or the laborious report. But change doesn't have to be loud to be legitimate. It can happen in whispers, in breaths, in one step turned in a slightly different direction than the one before. It can be expressed in a smile that hints at a new thought. It can be explained in a laugh that is a bit more genuine than before. But that's not even the point. It's not about how we can verify change, but the fact that change occurred when all odds were against it.

My imagination went back to the Red Sea and instead of looking back or forward, I looked at my feet. Miraculously, they were still walking on dry ground. I was not drowning. It was as if God was telling me that he had taken me this far and asking if I'd trust that He'd take me all the way through. Reflecting upon my hurt and healing, I recognized that "even though I walk through the valley of the shadow of death... [God was] with me; [His] rod and staff, they comfort me."[14] It's been a strange avenue for comfort. It's been a wild and feral place to exercise trust. I was changing here, ever so softly, ever so faintly.

During my last day in the alley that week, a warmth surrounded me. It was the dark cloud from Mount Sinai that wrapped around me, filling every place with a sense that someone else was with me, that someone else was holding me. I cautiously let my mind wander and found that my fears weren't as scary, my hurts just hurt a little less, and my brokenness seemed less broken. I realized I wasn't scared of this place anymore.

14. Ps 23:4.

# WEEK 4

# Finding Grace

I HAD A FANTASTIC imagination as a kid. In grade one, my best friend and I pretended we were rabbits in the wild, and we needed to create a burrow and a shelter for ourselves. We believed wholeheartedly that we would be able to dig under our school's shed to create our safe hideout. I remember going to a place called Turtle Hill on snowy days, equipped with cross country skis that my friend found in her garage. We would strap them on to go downhill skiing only to make it a couple of meters down the hill and get our feet and arms tangled up. We would laugh and roll our way to the bottom of the hill just to trudge back up and try again. I remember pretending that Rocket candies had superpower boosts that would help me bounce higher on a trampoline, or run faster down the field, or sing better than the birds around me. I remember creating a mini carnival in my basement with my sisters and brother, creating games and activities with what we had on hand to transport us to the amusement park of our dreams. My parents encouraged these wild adventures; they delighted in the crazy stories. They were glad to give us the space to make memories.

I remember being loved and feeling free. I remember the countless times that I would run into my house with bleeding knees or elbows from falling playing street hockey, tackle football, or basketball. My mom would pour hydrogen peroxide on scrapes, and it would make it hurt more, but I would still watch, fascinated, as the liquid would bubble and fizzle on my skin. I can still feel the warmth of my mom's hugs when I was cleaned up and ready to go out to play again. I remember when I was scared at night, my mom would come in, help me shut the curtains, tuck me in again while she listened to me try to explain my fears. She would always listen with care and compassion.

I remember having too many questions in my mind, and they needed to spill out of me. My dad had a chair that was designated for him and him alone. I remember sitting on his bony knees as he sat in his chair and asking him a thousand questions which he tried to answer, one by one. During Hockey Night in Canada, my dad would stretch out on the floor to watch the Canadian teams play, while snacking on peanuts. I would nestle myself behind his knees and watch and ask questions about the game, the team, the colors, the lines on the ice. I would ask about anything and everything. I was never told to be quiet. My dad always had time to explain why or how something worked.

Growing up, my mom was nurturing, creative, and loving; my dad was goofy, ambitious, and knowledgeable. We were a happy family. However, as I entered my middle and high school years, something shifted. I don't know if it was the stress of all the adolescent hormones coursing through our house or the lack of control my dad felt as one by one my siblings left for college. Maybe it happened when my dad lost his job, or when the tuition payments for school and college were getting larger and overwhelming. Perhaps, my parents had always had a hard time talking to each other, but as I spent the last two years of high school alone while my siblings were gone to college, I noticed the growing distance between my parents as they struggled to communicate over faith, family, and eventually even the basic day to day happenings. Maybe the shift happened because my dad was fighting his own inner battle, one that couldn't be explained outside of the confines of his own heart. I watched as the light that had always carried my family forward go out in my dad. It was snuffed out gradually and gently, so much

## WEEK 4: FINDING GRACE

so, that it was hard to pinpoint the time or the place, but he lost something of himself.

Where once it was easy to make my dad happy and proud, it became more difficult. He had always been a goal-oriented person, so simply accomplishing tasks, attaining goals, achieving to my potential was the ticket to his approval. I think I'm not alone in wanting to make my parents proud. Don't all kids want to do this? Don't we all just want to meet their expectations as a way of giving back to them, a way of letting them know their investment in us has good return? So, I worked hard to show my worth, to my dad in particular, through achievement. My dad wasn't a man that would publicly celebrate, or give an embarrassing bear hug, or excitedly ask about how an event went. He was a recluse, so he rarely witnessed the achievements, but he always heard about them. He would sit back in his chair in our living room, look at a report card or a certificate of accomplishment and a knowing nod and a large smile would encapsulate the pride he felt in the moment. I'd hear, on occasion, the words, "That's good." He was a reserved man, but I knew that he was celebrating inside of his heart.

But after his light went out, I felt like I needed to work harder for approval. My dad retreated so much into himself that he seemed to slowly close the doors on people around him. He'd open them up, once in a while, but I often felt like I was on the other side, stuck in the deafening silence. His silent treatments felt like rejection. His lack of response felt like abandonment. Despite all of my accomplishments and efforts, I constantly felt like I was disappointing him.

When I was growing up, I didn't understand love languages and the different ways people relate and show love to others. I didn't know how much my dad loved me because he showed it to me through acts of service. I didn't realize the depth of his love and that he would have done all the paperwork, behind the scenes work, late-night phone calls, and money arranging so that I could thrive. I didn't know that's what love can look like, and I wish I did. I spent a large portion of my teenage years just wanting a hug from him, wanting him to look in my eyes and say that he loved me no matter if I accomplished my goals or not, wanting him to be the dad who told me he was proud of me simply because I was his daughter. I wish I had searched for his love outside of my narrow list because I realize that my dad told me that he loved me in a million different ways.

I started out at the dumpster that week staring at the side of a storage trailer that had the numbers 1418 written on the side. As I settled my mind, I kept repeating the name God the Father over and over again. I kept hearing Jesus' words, from weeks before, echo, "Have you met my dad?" I tried to get comfortable with these words on the tip of my tongue. God the Father, God the Father, God the Father. I repeated them until I didn't want to be by them anymore. The words hung in the air and didn't attach themselves to anything. The silent treatment of my own father became a metaphysical silent treatment from God. What could I bring to my heavenly Father that he could be proud of? I couldn't think of much. I felt like a disappointment, like a failure, like a mistake. This reckless line of thinking spiralled out of control in me, bringing me down ugly roads of regret. I saw all the things that God had placed in front of me, all sorts of opportunities that I had shied away from or rejected in my life. How many times had I let my fear and shame hold me back from what God had called me to do? All of who I was at that moment seemed so sadly inadequate. I wanted to show a paper of accomplishment to God, a certificate of achievement, something to show that I was worth his attention. But I had empty hands. How could I get his attention? How could God be proud of me?

Why was it that I was comfortable to be around Jesus, but shied away from God the Father? Why was it that I could surrender to the Spirit and see things, hear things, and understand things I couldn't on my own, but was unable to confidently walk into the presence of the Father? I liked being with Jesus because He was human, therefore, much more relatable, concrete, and down to earth (literally!). I could abandon myself to the Spirit because She's like air, like oxygen, the only way for me to breathe in the connection with Jesus from two thousand years ago. But God the Father was

## WEEK 4: FINDING GRACE

and is completely different than I am. He is unknowable, transcendent, so completely other than me and my surroundings. I kept asking: *Who am I? Who am I to You, God?* I was having a tough go at the Trinity Oneness because the head of their whole operation seemed locked behind the same door my dad had closed, and I was struggling to get an appointment.

I felt anger rise inside of me. I got up off the concrete. I started to pace along the path of garbage between the trailer, the dumpster, and the brick wall. Back and forth I went as I felt my emotions surge inside of me. I started rubbing my hands together as if I were getting ready for a fight. That's exactly what I wanted to do. I wanted a fight. I had a bone to pick with God. I wanted to let Him know that the system that He set up here was flawed. It didn't work. He couldn't be an intimate Father and also an omniscient God. They are not synonymous. They don't coincide.

All my life I've been told, with sweet smiles and Sunday school sing-song voices, that God the Father was loving and trustworthy. Then, in the same breath, I've been taught that God is impossible to please, that He is manipulative, and that He has the habit of abandoning us. Teaching me these contradictory sides to God was an accident. Really it was. I don't think my teachers and mentors meant to teach me that, but it spilt out of them in the way they lived and how they spoke. Nonetheless, it was a double standard I was shown, and I was tired of wondering when God would be nice and open the door, and when he would be judgemental and slam it in my face.

When I took a philosophy class in college, I was fascinated by Greek mythology and its ability to reveal and describe parts of our world through stories. Take, for example, the character of Sisyphus. As the story goes, King Sisyphus was punished by Zeus for being deceitful and was sentenced to an eternity of rolling a boulder uphill, only to have it roll back down, leaving him to roll it back up all over again.[1] I was drawn to this story because it explained the endless cycle of sin and repentance that I was stuck in. I felt like I woke up every morning to start a day full of downfalls,

---

1. Cartwright, "Sisyphus."

shortcomings, deceit and lies. Even when I tried to avoid doing anything wrong, the boulder of iniquities came barrelling down at me anyways. So, I spent my time repenting, begging for forgiveness, pushing that boulder up the hill towards God so he would be pleased with my act of repentance. If I could just get all my sin to God, He would be proud of me, and He would forgive me. But I could never make it to the top, and I would wake up the next day in the same predicament. The weight of my sin was too much to keep pushing uphill, and I was tired of trying to please a God that was impossible to please. There just seemed to be no way to make it to the top of the hill and stand in His presence with dignity.

There is another Greek mythological character named Tantalus. He was once allowed to be in the presence of Zeus, but after making some selfish decisions, he was banished from Zeus' table and was sentenced to stand in a pool of water under a fruit tree. Though this seemed like a wonderful place for Tantalus to be, he was stuck in a place where the fruit from the tree was just beyond his grasp, and the water below him receded every time he tried to take a drink. He was trapped in a place of longing. He was beating himself up over his actions, hoping for an unknown day when he might be able to enjoy fruit and water again.[2] I tried to ignore the striking similarity between this story and when Adam and Eve were taken out of Eden, but there were too many common threads. I tried to push out all the explanations I've been given over the years of how we eagerly wait for Jesus to come back again, for when God's going to finally invite us fully back in, for when the Holy Spirit won't be the substitute while we wait for the fullness of God's presence again. I tried to ignore the underlying thought that God has been a bit manipulative in how he's set up the living situation here on earth. I mean, what's stopping God from giving us all of Him right now? Why trap us in a place of longing? When He said he brought the Kingdom of Heaven to earth, did He just bring bits and pieces of it?

I was also drawn to the mythological story of Persephone. She was abducted by Hades to live in a world of darkness with little

---

2. Cartwright, "Tantalus."

## WEEK 4: FINDING GRACE

hope of finding her way out. She made the best of it, ruling the Underworld the way she wanted to. She was permitted, for two-thirds of the year, to rejoin her mother in the real world where she flourished and gave the world fertility and vegetative life. But, inevitably, she would have to go back to the darkness, away from her life sources.[3] I found this story not just a story of the cycle of seasons on earth, but the cycle of seasons of the Christian life. From the pulpit at church or the front of classrooms, the cycle of spiritual hills and valleys were foretold. I would be close to God and flourish, then I would be sucked into life's brokenness and be separated from Him. I would experience love and goodness then I would go back to living amongst evil and despair. I would experience this manic life like the psalmist David, who says, "Surely Your goodness and love will follow me all the days of my life, and I will dwell in the house of the LORD forever."[4] And, the next day I would echo his words, "How long, Lord? Will you forget me forever? How long will you hide your face from me?"[5] I don't like emotional and spiritual rollercoasters. Abandonment stings and smarts every single time.

I laid out these examples of inconsistencies before God. I spat out my annoyance at the pavement and stomped all over it. How can God be gracious and compassionate to me when I was never good enough, never close enough, never seen? In my anger, I drove away from the dumpster, glad to escape that unforgiving place.

My anger subsided into melancholy again when I went back to the dumpster the next day. My heart sank even further when I arrived and saw my meeting place. I didn't face graffiti this time, it was worse. Someone had decided to forego a proper washroom and had defecated underneath the trailer beside the dumpster. Piles of wipes littered the area and the flies were buzzing in a frenzy. The leftovers of a breakfast sandwich were scattered by the side of the brick wall where I usually sat, and I thought, momentarily, that I could skip the hour of solitude for one day. The excuse was

3. Cartwright, "Hades."
4. Ps 23:6.
5. Ps 13:1.

## 40 Days at a Dumpster

justifiable: I didn't have to sit beside human feces. I quickly pushed the desire to run out of my mind just in case it started to gain traction. The point of coming to this place was not to clean it up, but to see if God was present in the mess, even if it was messier than I would have liked. If the Spirit could show up in the external mess, then She just might show up in my internal mess as well. She proved that She was willing. So, I wedged myself up against the dumpster and sat in the stink. My heart felt weak. My hopes were being trampled. I felt disappointed with myself. For all the distance I had covered on this journey, for all the healing and health I had received, this week felt like I was retreating again. Even though I had chosen life, I felt like I was dying. My progression towards the other side of this all seemed impossible. I couldn't find the key to open the door to the Father.

My imagination wandered towards the disciple Peter. I found him following Jesus who was being led to be questioned by the high priest. Someone started a fire in the courtyard, and Peter sat down with a small crowd of people warming themselves. Then, he did what he said he would never do. Out of protection, out of preservation, and for the sake of anonymity, Peter denied knowing Jesus when people confronted him on it. He had devoted his last three years of life, day in and day out, to Jesus, but in a lively campfire debate, Peter suddenly declared Jesus a stranger, unknown to him. Then the rooster crowed and, only in the gospel of Luke do we read that, "The Lord turned and looked straight at Peter. Then Peter remembered the word the Lord had spoken to him: 'Before the rooster crows today, you will disown me three times.' And he went outside and wept bitterly."[6] While my mind imagined this scene, I stepped into the shoes of Peter. I experienced his emotional confusion, trapped between what he wanted to do and what he didn't do. But what stopped my heart on that August morning was the look that Jesus gave us. Somehow during the questioning and debate with the high priest, there was a moment that happened in slow motion, as Jesus turned and looked straight into the eyes of Peter and me.

6. Luke 22:61–62.

## WEEK 4: FINDING GRACE

Every gospel states that Peter went outside and wept bitterly after this scene. Naturally, I thought it was because of Peter's shame, his embarrassment, and his fear of what the Lord must have thought of him. I always understood this passage as one where God pointed his finger at Peter and declared, "You disappoint me." Come to think of it, there were a lot of stories where I pictured God saying that: Adam and Eve in the Garden of Eden, David when he was caught in adultery, Tamar when she pretended to be a prostitute to have a child, Jonah when he threw a tantrum and didn't want to go to Ninevah, John Mark when he deserted Paul and Barnabas on a ministry road trip, and the list goes on. I etched my name on the list for all the times that I seemed to wholeheartedly give my heart to God only to relinquish it when I drummed up my list of insufficiencies. "You disappoint me," was all I heard.

But that day at the dumpster, the look Jesus gave me didn't send out that message. Maybe I have seen that campfire scene all wrong. I was so blinded by my own interpretation of myself, that I hadn't ever considered Jesus' interpretation of me or Peter. The situation challenged a biblical stance I had believed all my life that perhaps wasn't a truth at all. Nowhere, in any of these passages did God say he was disappointed. As I questioned this look Jesus gave me, I was reminded of His character. I don't think it was in Jesus to mockingly give an "I told you so," look. I don't think Jesus had the manipulative sass of a teenager to say in a look and a matching melodramatic sigh, "I knew I couldn't count on you." Was that in His nature? Was that what He was trying to say in that look? Because that's not the message I received.

When I saw Jesus look straight at me, His look penetrated through all of my layers of doubt, disgust, and disdain for myself and found my heart. It was a look of true compassion, of deep love, of reckless mercy, and . . . grace. It was the kindling that started a fire inside of me that I was unable to start myself. The look said *I see you, and I still love you.* Maybe that is why Peter wept so bitterly. After denying Jesus, not once, but three times, Jesus was able to look past all of that circumstantial rubbish and saw Peter the way God saw him: someone who was still loved despite the tragic circumstances. Maybe his tears fell with the words, "He didn't shun me or turn away. He still sees me and loves me even after what I've done." When Jesus looked at us, we didn't just understand unconditional love, we *experienced* it.

Full of self-consciousness, I admit that I have denied myself this type of love for a very long time. I wanted love to work within my system of rules and abide by my conditions. I wanted love to make sense, have measurables, and be given and received in a particular way. To be honest, Jesus' penetrating look was not part of my checklist. Being noticed without merit, being given value without criteria, being loved without limit wasn't a part of my paradigm. And so, rejecting love was a bad habit of mine. Jesus called me out on it and pressed me to accept a new set of rules.

That's when I thought back to the door that stood between my dad and me and the one I imagined God stood behind. It dawned on me that I had never checked to see if the door was shut. I had assumed that they had closed it, but maybe it had been open just a crack the entire time. Was it possible that they had been on the other side, anticipating the moment when I would put aside my rules and regulation for love, and just walk through the door into their way of showing it?

When I started up my van to leave the alley that morning, my phone rang and one of my sons was on the other end. "When are you coming home?" he asked. "I'm lonely."

I asked him, "How can you be lonely? You have your brother and sister with you."

He replied, "I know they are here. But, I need a mom with me."

"I'm coming home," I responded.

Besides melting my heart, my son gave me the words I wanted to say to God the Father but was too scared to voice. I whispered them out anyways. *I'm lonely God. I know I have my husband and kids and friends, even Jesus and the Spirit. But, I need the Father with me.* I let the request linger for a moment then I drove home to be with my son.

The morning sun of the next day was blocked out by clouds. By the dark and dreary dumpster, I took some time to reflect on the messy thoughts that had bubbled out of me during the week. I can only attribute my confusion about God's character to my devotion to the scientific proofs of cause and effect. My life has operated out of the "you-get-what-you-deserve" philosophy. My actions, therefore, are a result of desperately wanting what I deserve: faith when my frameworks make sense, hope when I've proven integrity and character, and love when I have done enough to earn it. I've also lived in a way to avoid what I don't deserve: mercy when I know I have done wrong, peace when others around me are suffering, and grace when I haven't done anything worthy of such reward. It's as if I started reading my Reformed theology book and came across the idea of total depravity and forgot to read further. If I was so broken, then I didn't deserve anything better, and I could expect nothing less. That's what I understood as justice. That was my expectation for order. But out of the 16th century, a profound and ancient thought surfaced: *sola gratia*, (Latin for *by grace alone*). These were two small words that I heard a thousand and one times, but they were so hard for me to understand because they didn't fit anywhere in the framework of my life. I didn't have space for this idea of being made flawless by grace alone when all around me screamed out that becoming better was done by grit and hard work alone. I was searching for a place within my mind or heart to reintroduce this word called "grace," but realized it would be impossible to bring that word into a place that was so hostile against it.

    Maybe that was the whole point of this emptying experience. I embarked on this journey by emptying my thoughts and feelings to make room for God. Now, He was challenging me to empty the most barricaded part of me, my heart, to make more room. He was asking me to throw out my checklist of standards and systems that religion and church and well-meaning people had made for me. How many years had I tried to check all the right boxes to earn God's favor and love? How well had it been working out for me? Justin Holcomb, an Episcopal priest, author and teacher, describes grace as "the love of God shown to the unlovely; the peace of God given to the restless; the unmerited favor of God."[7] I had

---

7. Holcomb, "What is Grace?," para. 2.

no defence for this type of love. I had no way to fight it off. With a stare straight from Jesus, I was given an old word as if it was a new gift for me to open. When I asked why He was trying to give it to me once again, He replied with a smile, *Just because*. He waited for me to unwrap it, clear some space inside, and place it at and over the doorframe of my heart.

Helen Keller, at 19 months old, became deaf and blind. I can't even imagine not being able to communicate with others and not being able to understand anything in the dark world around me. She was so full of anger and fury at the world that her parents decided to find help to control her. Anne Sullivan, a teacher specializing in blind students, came to teach Helen how letters became words, and how words identified objects. In her darkened world, where nothing made sense, Anne's attempts to provide the meaning of words and life seemed futile. It seemed so disconnected to Helen's reality. Helen memorized the words but couldn't link the words with her existence.

Then, one day, Anne and Helen were by a water pump. With Helen's hands feeling the water, Anne spelt the word "water" into her hand. In her autobiography, Helen Keller wrote about that day:

> As the cool stream gushed over one hand she spelt into the other the word water, first slowly, then rapidly. I stood still, my whole attention fixed upon the motions of her fingers. Suddenly I felt a misty consciousness as of something forgotten—a thrill of returning thought, and somehow the mystery of language was revealed to me. I knew then that 'w-a-t-e-r' meant the wonderful cool something that was flowing over my hand. That living word awakened my soul, gave it light, hope, joy, set it free! There were barriers still, it is true, but barriers that could in time be swept away.[8]

The word "grace," became Helen Keller's "w-a-t-e-r" to me. At the dumpster of all places, sitting next to someone's shit and rotting breakfast sandwiches, the word "grace" made its home inside of me, awakened my soul, and continued untangling the ropes

---

8. Dilnawaz, "On This Day," para. 6.

## WEEK 4: FINDING GRACE

of depravity, self-hatred, and fear that were wrapped around me. Grace cleared out a narrow passage through all the self-defeating thoughts I had hoarded over the years and told me that I didn't have to roll boulders, or reach for fruit, or go away from His presence. Cause-and-effect philosophy drifted away in importance, and grace gave me a thin avenue to walk to God, my Father. I tentatively walked through the passage towards this Heavenly Father whom I had been afraid to see.

I had noticed the numbers 1418 on the trailer in front of me at the beginning of the week. It was almost the end of the week, and I glanced at them again. On a whim, I looked up the passage John 14:18 and started reading the section. It seemed like many of the Scriptures that came to my mind here in the alley were from the book of John, so I thought that might be a good place to look. While I was pushing Jesus and the Spirit aside, looking for God the Father, He had laid out the answer for me to receive when I was ready. Jesus said,

> "I will not leave you as orphans; I will come to you. Before long, the world will not see me anymore, but you will see me. Because I live, you also will live. On that day you will realize that I am in my Father, and you are in me, and I am in you. . . *He who loves me will be loved by my Father, and I too will love him and show myself to him.*" [italics added][9]

On that day, I realized I didn't have to search for my heavenly Father and provide a certificate of worth and accomplishment to Him. I didn't have to earn a time slot with Him. He had been with me the whole time through Jesus. God was One and the same with Son and Spirit. In revealing my brokenness, hurt and wounds to Jesus, I had already dropped the compulsion to hide my insufficiencies. My worst fear, that God would turn me away, never transpired. In fact, I think the Triune God likes me—even loves me—just as I am.

Of all the places this epiphany could happen, it happened here. I found grace in the garbage.

---

9. John 14:18–21.

# WEEK 5

# Grace—The Finality of Life

I WENT TO THE dumpster sleepy and groggy the first day of the week. I was trying to settle my mind, but my thoughts were scattered everywhere like a game of Pick Up 52. I didn't know if I should collect them, push them individually aside, or just sit right in the middle of them. Like a deck of cards, my mind was jumping between four categories: my mental capacity to process this journey, my emotional stability in dredging up wounds and scars, my physical stamina to repeat the same routine every morning, and my relational responsibilities outside of this alley of being a mom and wife. Within each of those avenues of thought were even more details to scrutinize and dissect. Considering how tired I was, I just plopped myself right on top of my thoughts and the concrete and leaned back on the cold metal of the dumpster. I saw a distorted mirror image of myself in the metal of the trailer in front of me. I can't even say if I could make out an image, with all the rust and knobs, pipes and diamond-plated sheet metal. I saw the form of my reflection, but that's about it. I sat for about half an hour, listlessly on the ground. I was neither able to function inwardly to fight my fears, nor was I able to operate outwardly and make eye contact with the two strangers that started to approach me, hesitated, then hurried away. Finally, my brain stopped trying to distract me, and I was left to sit in a place of nothingness.

## WEEK 5: GRACE — THE FINALITY OF LIFE

I closed my eyes and slowly gained some bearings. I found myself on a mountain, yet the scenery was different than the dark cloud of Mount Sinai. I was at Mount Tabor, sitting a small distance away from Jesus' disciples Peter, James, and John. They, too, looked sleepy as their eyes were all half-mast. They huddled around a rock, unaware that I was on the other side. I looked out at the plains surrounding this mountain and marvelled at how the desert seemed to stretch out as far as the sky. This mountain seemed like an interruption to the endless land, an abnormality to the normal around it. Anticipation started to form inside my heart as I could sense that what I was about to encounter would be an interruption to the dry and endless landscape of my soul too. I had a premonition that this change in mountain terrain, from Sinai to Tabor, would be a change of experience too.

As the three disciples and I sat on the mountain watching Jesus from a couple of meters away, I felt the juxtaposition of being hidden and exposed. I knew I was not seen by anyone, but I felt like the foul parts of me were out in plain view. I looked down at my hands and saw that, for no good reason, they looked a little distorted. They were crooked and had a strange yellow hue to them. Startled at their appearance, I started examining the rest of my body and found that my skin looked puffy, as if I had been in water for a while. My wrists, arms and shoulders had large gashes across them, cuts that looked as if I had been running through a dense forest. My shirt was ripped, my jeans were scuffed, my shoes were torn. I looked as if I had been in a fight that I definitely did not win. I drew my knees up to my chin in an attempt to hide the wounds from the open air. I tried to cover up how disfigured I looked and to hide the sudden vulnerability I felt.

I peeked over my knees and looked out at Jesus and found that He was talking with two other men. My mind knew the story of who he was with: Moses and Elijah. I knew they were talking about Jesus' upcoming crucifixion. But then I was brought into parts of the story that I hadn't encountered in Scripture. As the sound of their voices drifted to my ears, I was surprised to be able to understand their conversation in English, but also fascinated by the frequency that the word "exodus" came up. What I once thought was a word reserved for and trademarked by the Israelite experience was now being used by these men as a common word. They were using the word to describe Jesus' departure, His anticipated journey, His lonely road to walk. The word so easily described the common theme of leaving and transition throughout the Biblical narrative: Adam and Eve's leaving Eden, the Israelites flight from Egypt, Naomi and Ruth's trek from Moab, the disciples' following an unconventional rabbi and Jesus' journey of carrying the cross up the route of the *Via Dolorosa* towards his crucifixion. "Exodus" was a word that even described my place here at the dumpster. I knew I had left a previous understanding of myself and was on a lonely road of discovering what would be my true identity.

As I looked at Jesus, awe overwhelmed me, and I became mesmerized. The other two men had faded in the mist of clouds while Jesus was physically transforming before my eyes. At first, I saw all the colors of the rainbow dance together over, above and through Him. Yellow twirled into purple, purple leapt into green, green slid into red and red fell into blue. Their brilliance pulsated to the beat of His heart and then, all at once, the colors burst into an immaculate pure white light. It looked as if Jesus was draped in a robe of living light. Millions of white photons shimmered around Him, his clothes taking on the energy of something transcendent and wholly other than the earth He stood on. It was fascinating. It was awe-inspiring. The energy and light kept spilling over and splashing around Him. I looked over at Peter, James and John and saw their faces reflecting the brilliance of the Spirit herself. I saw a stream of light trickling like a babbling brook towards me. I reached out to play with the energy and watched all the distortions of my body, all the sores change and transform. They didn't disappear; they seemed to adjust—to soften and smooth over—letting the light move over and through them fluidly. My body jolted with energy as if every part of my body was given a boost of vitality. I heard words rise from the depths of light: *This my Son, whom I love. Listen . . .*

## WEEK 5: GRACE—THE FINALITY OF LIFE

My eyes flew open, and I was back in the alley. With wide eyes, I tried to make sense of the vision I just experienced. I felt an instantaneous sting like I had just been burned and frozen at the same time. The heat made its way into me and slowly warmed me to my core, and the cold became a revitalizing breeze giving me fresh air. I tried to process what had just occurred at Mount Tabor. How did I go from being disfigured to being transfigured with Jesus? How did all of me seem to switch from one extreme to another? Sitting here nothing changed, yet everything changed. I felt different, and I felt the same. I couldn't make sense of it, but I was driven to try.

It was like I was given a riddle to solve, a word game to play. I looked up the prefix "dis," as in disfigure, and discovered that it meant *apart* or *away*.[1] That's just it: I've spent so much time looking at myself apart from God. In trying to be in control, in trying to solve everything on my own, thinking I've needed to clean myself up before I meet with Him, I've wandered too often away from God. No wonder I saw myself as disfigured. Apart from God, I'm the wilted fig tree, the dying branch, the seed choked out by weeds. I seem to voluntarily cut myself off from my life-source all the time like Robert Robinson wrote in his hymn "Come Thou Fount of Every Blessing," *"Prone to wander Lord I feel it, prone to leave the God I love."*[2]

But on Mount Tabor, transfiguration occurred. The prefix "trans" means *across*, or my favorite, *changing thoroughly*.[3] Jesus went "across" in so many ways, across from divine to mortal, from teacher to criminal, from respected to despised, from rejected to glorified. What was truly astounding, was that His definition of change was so different from mine. To me, change involved discarding something old and embracing something new. Jesus' transformations didn't throw out the old but mysteriously embraced both the former while becoming the latter too. He didn't leave his divine nature to become mortal; His divinity and mortality became

1. Dictionary.com, s.v. "dis-."
2. Robinson, "Come Thou Fount," 486.
3. Dictionary.com, s.v. "trans-."

unified. He didn't cease his role as teacher to become an outlaw; His best lessons came from his pursuit of perfect justice. He didn't lose the respect of his followers when he was tortured; He gained honor in the depth of despair. He didn't brush off rejection when He resurrected; He demonstrated how exclusion and inclusion can occur simultaneously. I saw Him change completely, and by Him, I saw myself transform too. I've always loved the matter-of-factness of change in the transfiguration story: Jesus was human, and Jesus was divine. No further explanation needed. In my vision, I caught a quick glimpse of the pure mystery of who Jesus actually was and is when He isn't restricted by assumptions and logic. On that day at the dumpster, I also caught a glimpse of who I was actually made to be. I was no longer disfigured and apart, but I was transfigured and changed over. I was a wounded and broken human, and I was intimately connected and redeemed in the same eternal moment.

Belden Lane had a similar experience in understanding the transfiguration story in a new way. As Lane physically trod up Mount Tabor on a late February day, he was struck by the lush beauty of the mountain that stood on its own in the middle of a vast plain by Megiddo, Israel. While alone at the top of the mountain, he read through the account of the transfiguration from the gospel of Matthew. Sitting there, He wrote,

> Dark clouds were gathering, I knew that in taking this time alone I was probably also missing a ride back down the mountain with some of those who'd come for Mass. But the words of the gospel went right through me as I stumbled over the passage. I heard them spoken by God not only to Jesus but also, it seemed, to me. "You are my son," the voice was saying, "the one I love. I'm pleased with you; I take pleasure in who you are. Listen (and attend carefully) . . .to my glory within you" (Matt. 17:5) . . . I couldn't get away from the embarrassed, almost heretical feeling that in all my ordinariness—a foreigner with cold feet and anxiousness about the weather—I was somehow in that moment included in the transfiguring light once revealed in that place.[4]

4. Lane, *Solace of Fierce Landscapes*, 132.

## WEEK 5: GRACE—THE FINALITY OF LIFE

Later in his book, he described the similarities of his experience to the ancient way of understanding the passages of Scripture referring to the transfiguration of Jesus:

> While [my] reading of the text may seem presumptuous to Western ears, I'd learn later that it follows exactly the Greek fathers' understanding of the transfiguration event. The disciples' vision of Jesus deified human flesh on Mount Tabor revealed to them not only the glory of God, but also what it means most fully to be human. Part of their amazement at the transfiguration was that, in seeing Jesus, they also saw themselves anew.[5]

This was the unexpected yet beautiful grace that I was given in the back alley that was adorned with rust and sludge: that while I felt dead, I was very much alive; while I was stained by my past, I was pure in the present; while I was ordinary, I was extraordinary. I understood that I was created to live traversing across the great divide of being cast out of Eden and brought across to the New Jerusalem. I found a strange peace in that chasm as if I were meant to find comfort in the uncomfortable. I couldn't deny the hard experiences of living my life, but I also couldn't dismiss the very real understanding that I was tasting pieces of heaven with every step. With one foot in the mire and the other foot on solid ground, I was slowly embracing my own transfiguration.

High on the euphoria of the vision, I went home. I still couldn't make full sense of it all. My thoughts were still scattered in my head. I received something resembling new life and hope that day, and I was desperate to hold onto it.

The next day, I sat again and thought about the day before. I was astounded by how vivid and tangible the stream of the Spirit was for me. It was as if I could still reach out and feel her electrifying presence cascade over me. I was in danger of thinking that God, Jesus, and the Spirit were changing and performing for me as if I were the constant, and all of these experiences were the unveiling of the evolution of the Trinity. Thinking I was a mere member of the audience, while the spiritual show played before

---

5. Lane, *Solace of Fierce Landscapes*, 132.

me, would bring me back to where I was before. It would throw me back to the start of this journey where I believed that I was in control and that God would play on my terms. The reality was that God doesn't change—it was me that had been changing. God was not the fickle one. I was. He was the same God who created the world, who thought of me before I was born, who held me in the alley, who healed me on my path, who loved me and loves me and always will. He is the unchanging one. My circumstances didn't change Him, but were changed *by* Him. That, I realized, was what life looks when grace invades. Grace made my heart bend, buckle, mold, and change over.

It had rained overnight, and the clouds were threatening to release their waters again. The stench coming up from the dumpster was terrible. It was a mix of wet Doritos, soggy pizza boxes, fermenting food and feces. I gagged but forced myself to stay. Even though the smell was nauseating, all the other things here that once offended me were now the constants that I sought out. There was the crow that kept throwing pieces of pinecones and tree pieces at me from atop the trailer. There were delivery trucks that came and went but were always tight to their schedules. I saw the postal service guy back up his small delivery van just a couple of meters away from where I sat. The man with the burgundy backpack would walk the sidewalk to the road halfway through my time here. The two coffee-drinking, cigarette-smoking friends sat on a bench across the parking lot. On occasion, there was another man who carried a plastic bag full of empty cans who wandered the alleyway and would meet up with his friends by the bench. All of this was part of the rhythm, part of the liturgy of this place. Perhaps the stench was even a part of the routine I had come to expect. On days like this one, where nothing in particular happened inside or out, the constants around me kept me sane.

After Moses finished hearing God's Ten Commandments, maybe there was a lull. After Jonah was spat out of the whale, maybe there was a chance to catch his breath. After Jesus was tempted in the desert the first time, maybe there was a couple of days grace before the next temptation was given. Even in heaven, "When [the

## WEEK 5: GRACE—THE FINALITY OF LIFE

Lamb] opened the seventh seal, there was silence in heaven for about half an hour."[6] After such vivid encounters with Jesus and transfiguration, maybe the past couple days of nothingness were my blessed break as well. It was my chance to let Her light settle into my wounds.

Psychiatrist and psychoanalyst C.G. Jung once wrote, "I am not what has happened to me. I am what I choose to become."[7] I think I started this journey fully believing and trusting that all of whom I have become has been rooted in what had happened to me. I believed, wrongly, of course, that rape and all the lies that emerged from that experience blocked me from God's full grace. Initially, I think I was looking for mercy here. I wanted to see if God would be kind enough to spare me from further pain, disappointment, and sadness if I raised my white flag and laid it all out in front of Him. I thought that I could pay my indulgence with time spent here, God would whisk all the pain away, and I would be free from eternal agony. But through old stories seen in new ways, He gave me more than I expected and provided an area to practice what courage could look like when I stepped out of my past and used the voice He gave me. I had been repeating the words spoken to me by a stranger twenty years ago as I was left in a dirty alley, "You are worthless, and nobody cares if you live or die." God, for weeks and in a long journey of silence, had led me gently out of those words and gave me the choice to step into something new. I had been asked to choose between life and death seemingly hundreds of times during the mornings spent at the dumpster. I had been asked to serve either the Divine King or the Wanna-Be King. Just as Elijah asked the Israelites at Mount Carmel whom they would serve, God asked me yet again, *"How long will you go limping between two opinions? If the LORD is God, follow Him."*[8] God was patient, compassionate, slow to anger, and *persistent*. Every time He asked, the urgency increased. I started to understand that even though it was my decision to make, He was holding me

---

6. Rev 8:1.
7. Medrut, "Carl Jung Quotes," para. 1.
8. 1 Kgs 18:21.

and guiding me through the choice over and over again. There was a new assurance that He was on both sides of the decision, always with me. Something was soothing, like the energetic water and light that flowed through me at Mount Tabor in understanding His omnipresence. That, yes, it was my decision. It was up to me to choose what I would become. Thank God that He helped me out in that decision. Thank God, that He took my feeble and frail "yes" and turned it into a song. So, whenever I return to those words that have defined me—and I inevitably will—I hope that the song will replay over in my mind, haunting me with its lyrics of love and acceptance.

I've been wired to be a rationalist, a natural cynic. I like proofs, formulas, diagrams, and flowcharts. At the dumpster, I have learned to let my guard down and become comfortable with God's untethered nature. I have found that God is good without Him having to show His goodness all the time. But He still chooses to. I have noticed that God is faithful without having to prove it incessantly. But He still does. I know that God is forever merciful without having to go to the unlikely places and extend it. Yet, His fingerprints are here. I've experienced that God is the giver of grace without needing to explain or rationalize it. *And He never will.* Grace is annoying like that. Everything else is in the proofs, the evidence, the confirmation. But grace just exists alone . . . *sola gratia*.

John, while introducing Jesus, gave away the ending before he even told his story. In the very first chapter of his book, John pointed directly at Jesus, and I imagine him telling everyone within earshot, "This guy is the one I've been telling you all about the whole time! He is God. He is the One. Through Him, and because of Him, this world is going to transform! How? Through the absurd truth of grace." John wrote in his gospel, "Out of his fullness we have all received grace in place of grace already given"[9] Without holding back, Jesus is going to keep giving grace to replace the grace I already had. What's that even mean? If I've already been given the gift of grace, why does He give me the replacement part?

9. John 1:16.

## WEEK 5: GRACE—THE FINALITY OF LIFE

Does this mean that my old grace has gone bad? Does grace run out? Does it run dry?

I had kept my journey more or less to myself all of those weeks. My husband, my pastor, and my close friends were the only ones privy to the knowledge. At first, I believed that I was keeping it hidden for privacy, but I think that I didn't tell anyone else because I didn't have an explanation of why I needed to take that journey. In my exodus, I had been afraid to explain that I had been walking *with* God because it might be understood as walking *away* from Him. Did my need to spend time at the dumpster mean that I had lost faith? That everything I held sacred before the dumpster experience was null? Did it mean that my previous faith was a fake? As I traced my fingers in the rust stains on the ground, I was afraid to admit to myself and to others that I had run dry. I had not left God; I was just parched and afraid of dying alone. Then John spoke up from centuries ago, and I was given what I didn't know I needed: grace in place of the grace that was depleted. While I walked through the dry vast plains of desert emptiness, I drank from grace's deep waters and my canteen ran low. He gave me more grace. While I climbed up the rugged mountainside of my past, slipping on the loose rock, my canteen of grace ran low again. He gave me more. As I entered the darkest cloud of unknowing, the air itself seemed to lap up every trace of grace I had in my pack. Again, He gave me more. How many times had He given me more? I didn't keep track, but I know that every time I realized I was thirsty, I was given something to drink. Alexander MacLaren, on his exposition of this verse, writes,

> The Evangelist's idea seems to be that as one supply of grace is given and used, it is, as it were given back to the Bestower, who substitutes for it a fresh and unused vessel, filled with new grace. . . Just as a careful gardener will stand over a plant that needs water, and will pour the water on the surface until the earth has drunk it up, and then add a little more; so He gives step by step, grace for grace, an uninterrupted bestowal, yet regulated

according to the absorbing power of the heart that receives it."[10]

I like that image of grace being absorbed by my heart. This image replaces the picture I had seen for years. I had always understood "receiving grace" as a one-time event that brings someone from unbelief into belief. But grace doesn't end there. It is the stream of light and energy from God, that trickled and tumbled over all of creation to me, and gives me the power of grace to live every day. It's not a matter of if I will absorb it, but how much I will abandon myself into it each day.

I showed up for my 34th day at the dumpster, and I wondered to myself why I was still coming back here. Surely by now, I'd be sick of this place. Surely by now, the allure of the adventure was over. Surely by now, the monotony would be killing me. Surely by now, I'd have learned enough. But I couldn't believe the distance I had travelled in this desert. I also didn't realize how subtle a drastic change could look. I didn't know how exile would bring the unexpected companion of the Spirit, Her dark cloud connecting me to Jesus and the Father in ways I didn't know were possible. But I do know that I had somehow crossed over, transfigured in a way that was illogical and wonderfully confusing. This time, I didn't even want to understand it. I just wanted to live here on the other side.

Just as I kept coming back to the dumpster, a place that once represented hurt and woundedness, I wondered how many times Mary and John went back to the cross. The alley was not a typical place to find grace, nor would a hill of torture be one. I kept coming back because I was drawn to the transformation it signified. I like to think that Mary and John had the same nostalgic desire to go back to the unlikely place of victory too. It's where inexpressible pain was overpowered by surprising love. This place of death was my journey of resurrection. I like to picture Mary and John exchanging a knowing look with each other as if they too were let in on the scandalous truth of grace given in place of grace.

10. MacLaren, "Expositions of Holy Scripture."

# WEEK 6

# Grace—The Finality of Death

I WAS GOING ON my sixth week at the dumpster. I was getting restless, mostly because I knew what I was doing was unnatural and not sustainable. I couldn't keep coming here every day, but I didn't know when I would be done. Just as God had shown me that I had to stay, I was trusting that He would show me when to leave. There would be an end to this exile, to my desert wandering.

I sat once again in my familiar spot to empty myself. At first, this process was freeing up space from my narrow-minded thoughts. I just had to empty my plans for the day, my regrets over letting my kids have extra screen time yesterday, my fears that something will go wrong at home during this hour away, my doubts that what I was doing made any sense, and my curiosity over the next section of the book I was reading. Having walked in this desert though, this wasteland had created so many more thoughts and emotions and questions than I had anticipated. I was emptying myself of everything prior to this journey, and now I had to empty my thoughts of this journey itself. I was distracting myself with the desert sand, the heat, the mirages of the journey's completion. I was looping back in my mind to all the places I had been, internally dreading where I might be taken this week. There was no compromise here; I had to stumble forward with nothing in tow. As Henri Nouwen wrote,

Our temptation is to do something useful: to read something stimulating, to think about something interesting, or to experience something unusual. But our moment of solitude is precisely a moment in which we want to be in the presence of our Lord with empty hands, naked, vulnerable, useless, without much to show, prove, or defend. That is how we slowly learn to listen to God's small voice."[1]

So, I emptied and sat in nothingness once again. I wanted to hear the Father, Son, and Spirit again. In visions, in thoughts, in ideas, in Scripture, in silence—however they wanted to show up.

When my brain, my soul, and my spirit held onto nothing, I closed my eyes and found myself sitting beside the empty tomb. I heard the excited chatter from a group of women trying to spit out the fact that Jesus' body was gone. They kept stammering over the word "resurrection" as they hurried away, likening the situation to Lazarus. The guards were taking off in a mixture of fear and anger, no doubt to tell the authorities that Jesus' body no longer lay in the tomb. Everyone was rushing away from where I sat, and the dust slowly settled to the ground in front of me. I was stuck wondering why I was still sitting while everyone else was running. Why wasn't I a part of the entourage telling people of life? Why wasn't I in the excited conversations with people telling them of Jesus? Of resurrection? Of grace? But I was not with the crowd. I was at the empty tomb because grace wasn't done with me yet.

I felt compelled to walk into the tomb, so I sat on the cold stone where Jesus' body had been. I sucked in the stale air, my heart pounding as I sat on His deathbed. I had an overwhelming need to stay here and say goodbye. It felt like such a silly and foolish thought, but I felt like I had to say goodbye to all the things that I assumed were already dead. Why would I have to say goodbye to these past hurts, traumas, misunderstandings, and selfish thoughts when I had laid them at the cross? I had already watched my past die in so many ways. I'd nailed papers representing my sin to a cross at the front of a church. I'd used tacks to pin up my regrets on

---

1. Nouwen, *Making All Things New*, 76–77.

## WEEK 6: GRACE—THE FINALITY OF DEATH

corkboard crosses at the front of classrooms. I'd lit candles to represent my prayer of sacrifice to God. I'd thrown sugar in bonfires at camps to symbolize the release of my sins to Christ at the cross. Even here at the dumpster, I'd seen Jesus carry my burdens and my shame. I'd crucified my sins and brokenness over and over again. Why did I have to say goodbye?

Sitting on the dusty stone in the empty tomb I realized that watching something die was different from laying something to rest and saying goodbye. Jesus' death on the cross was a different event than when they wrapped His body and laid Him in the tomb. I was just beginning to understand the importance of separating the two because it made a difference at resurrection. I had been so eager to go from crucifixion straight to the resurrection. Paul writes to the Romans, "For if we have been united with him in a death like his, we will certainly also be united with him in a resurrection like his. For we know that our old self was crucified with him."[2] The problem for me is, after the agony of watching Jesus die, I want to resurrect Him right away. And there is this union, like Paul wrote, between Jesus and me and the rest of the world. So, right after the flurry of throwing my sins at the cross and witnessing their demise, I rush to be resurrected right alongside Jesus. In that process though, I've been accidentally resurrecting my past hurts along with me, as if I didn't notice that I was still lugging them along. When I look at the crucifixion process and the process of entombment—of preparing Jesus body for its final rest—there were three long days for everyone to say goodbye. There was no rush to resurrection because no one was anticipating it. I guess I was feeling the need to hold a funeral of sorts, an entombment for death itself. I had to lay my old self to rest and be given the chance to leave it in the tomb. I needed to be able to have time and space to physically walk away and say, *I'm done with you. It is, really, finished.*

I came back to the alley and the tomb the next day, not sure how to hold a funeral for all the things that I didn't want to bring to life again. All the funerals I have attended celebrate the life, the achievements, and the heart of someone. Every memorial I've been

2. Rom 6:5.

to, even for the most difficult of people, highlight their good qualities while noticing their difficulties and then the officiant would go on and explain how they will not experience pain or hardship any longer. But, that's not the case here. The things I nailed to the cross are not things to remember with fondness. At the cross, I needed them to die, totally and with finality. I didn't want death and sin to sting me anymore. So, I was stuck. How was I supposed to say goodbye? For the entire hour, I tried to push the thought out, but it kept resurfacing.

I sent a message to my pastor asking him for some advice. I asked him, "Have you ever had to lead a funeral for a scumbag? For a truly horrible person?" I realized that my questions personified my wounds and heartache. Without context I asked him a misleading question: I asked him to advise me on how to reconcile, in my heart, the death of an individual. In my defence, over the past twenty years, my hurts have haunted me like a persistent being rather than an objective event. So, I felt the need to treat them as such. My pastor responded that evening, "Yes. I've done a funeral for a gang member who was murdered after he collected for a drug deal. I talked about unfinished business—we all have unfinished business at the end of our lives. Only Jesus can finish our unfinished business." He then commented, "As a preacher at a funeral, I concentrate on declaring the gospel because if I focus too much on just saying nice things about the person that can get difficult—as in the person you may be talking about." It was helpful advice. The "gospel of nice" I grew up with told me I should recognize how I "grew from the heartache" or how I "developed character through trials." But those statements gave the wound too much credit, too much power. My pastor's email helped me see that I didn't need to focus on the attributes of my hurt, as if I were trying to soften the blow for funeral attendees. I didn't have to glorify any part of the wound; rather, I was able to focus on my final step in surrender. In choosing life over death, I needed to give up my struggle to complete my unfinished business on my own. I had always felt that it was my responsibility to conquer the wound, to capture it, to imprison it, to hold the master keys that locked it in its place. But

## WEEK 6: GRACE—THE FINALITY OF DEATH

the truth was, conquering death was out of my realm of expertise. As long as I was vying for control, it would remain unfinished, and grace of resurrection with Christ would never be realized.

When Paul was trying to explain to the Corinthian church about the mystery of being resurrected with Christ, and how we are changed, he wrote "the saying that is written will come true: 'Death has been swallowed up in victory.' Where, O death, is your victory? Where, O death, is your sting?"[3]

When I read this verse, and when I picture the Corinthians hearing this, my mind relates it back to the Red Sea again. The Israelites thought death was on their heels with Pharaoh's army in hot pursuit. But then, as they crossed the Red Sea, they looked back and saw the army get swallowed up by the waters. I hear the disbelief, the gasp and then the victory cry. I imagine the Israelites hugging each other, half crying, half laughing, and stumbling over their thoughts as they marvelled at this saving grace, this amazing grace, this too-good-to-be-true grace. They just witnessed their imminent death being washed away, swallowed up, and spat onto the shoreline. It wasn't their plan, their idea, or their strategy. They didn't do anything except trudge through a dry seabed and make it to the other side. Just when they thought they wouldn't make it out alive, they came out without the slightest sting of assault on their backs. It made me believe that maybe I had a chance of coming out the other side here. I tasted the sweet finality of life the week prior; here was my chance to witness the finality of death.

As I sat in the alley, on the cement ledge next to the dumpster, on the stone seat of where Jesus body once lay, I realized I didn't have to perform the funeral. Again, how egotistical to think it was all up to me to make things happen. I, in fact, had walked into a funeral already in progress. I suspect this might be another one of those things that I will continually be asked to participate in. The song kept repeating faintly in the background of my mind, bouncing around the walls of the tomb, "Where, O death, is your victory? Where, O death, is your sting?" I felt a holy presence.

---

3. 1 Cor 15:54–55.

The Spirit danced up and around me, like the smoke of incense, circling and spiralling upward. She smelled earthy and warm and relaxed my anxious heart. She drew my eyes toward where Jesus' body had once been, and she brought out words in front of me. I can't even say they were written anywhere other than that the words hung in the air. The first ones that appeared were *Regret* and *Shame*. Images of memories came up in front of me as if I were peering through a window, a portal or a passageway into my experiences. I saw the regret of walking and talking with a stranger that would eventually hurt me. I saw the shame of rape and who I thought I was because of it. I saw the regret of all the opportunities I had been given in life, but couldn't walk into: educational opportunities, friendships that offered deep acceptance, people who needed to hear my story to know they weren't alone. I saw the shame I've carried into social gatherings where I felt unworthy to speak, to share, or to teach because of the scarlet letter that had been pinned to my coat. I saw my regret in all the hugs that were offered to me that could have retaught me the value of care and compassion, but I accepted rigidly or I rejected without explanation. I saw the shame in the countless times I tried to hurt myself to escape the pain, to numb the internal hurt, to ignore the hatred I felt for myself.

As I looked at each scenario, I felt a warm love stir inside of me. Without fully understanding the process, I let go of regret and shame and watched God's shadow overpower them. His dark cloud was thick and dense and swallowed the words up right before my eyes. He called out to me in the fog, *Step into your new identity.* I looked down and saw the footsteps of someone else, and I recalled how Moses was described in Hebrews 11: "Although he was raised as the son of Pharaoh's daughter, he refused to make that his identity."[4] A surge of determination welled up inside of me, and I stepped into Moses' dusty footprint. Rejecting who I thought I was, I stepped into the reality of who I was designed to be. I felt the warm embrace of grace's arms around me, singing into my ear words of encouragement and love. I watched my festering hurt and

---

4. Heb 11:24 (The Passion Translation).

## WEEK 6: GRACE—THE FINALITY OF DEATH

boiling self-hatred cool off with the touch of twilight, and I felt my open wounds become the scars of a new story of worth, belonging, and acceptance. Following ancient footsteps, I came down from Mount Sinai radiating the glory of being known and accepted.

The Spirit then brought out two more words, *Alone* and *Afraid*. She hung them as if they were large curtains then slowly drew them back to show another window into my past. I saw a small girl alone in my childhood bedroom, her feelings of isolation spilling out onto her bed and flooding the floor around her. I saw the fear of losing friends, uncles and aunts, grandparents, and my own parents to disasters and disease. I saw the sporting events I was in throughout high school and looking into the crowd hoping to see one of my parents witness my games, only to see the parents of other kids cheering me on. I saw the parties and social gatherings I attended—weddings, graduations, celebrations—that felt like dreams where I was there in physical form, but out of extreme anxiety and fear couldn't create a connection to those around me. I saw the attempts to describe the ache inside of me to others, to explain the pain in a place I couldn't locate, and I saw the confusion in people's eyes. I remember telling myself to just keep it all inside of me because it didn't make sense on the outside. I saw the condemnation from the church and leaders I respected over the years that taught me that the inner thoughts I had were sinful, selfish, and disappointing to God. I saw the fear in my eyes every time a self-destructive thought came because I didn't know where to dispose of it before God found out and walked away from me for good.

The Spirit seemed to gather up all those memories, and She poured water from the heavens overtop of them. Jesus stood on the waters and reached out His hand to me, beckoning me to join Him. I felt the strength of faith support me as I stepped onto the river to hold Jesus' hand. Similar to Ezekiel, where he saw water flow from the temple into the Dead Sea, I looked down into the waters and saw the memories that had brought death to me transfigure into new life. God had told Ezekiel, "when it empties into the sea, the salty water there becomes fresh. . . because this water flows there and makes the salt water fresh; so where the river flows everything will live."[5] In the clear waters, I saw the faces of select friends and my pastor who didn't shy away when the truth about me was out in the open. I saw the light in my dad's eyes when it returned 15 years ago, and I watched the snapshots of love and support lap up to my feet, wave after wave. As I stood with Jesus on the shimmering water, it was like I stood on Mount Tabor with Him and saw my past, present, and future change over from isolation to connection, from fear to peace.

And then She brought out the last of her words, *Emptiness* and *Hopeless*. It was as if She found the pit inside of me and drew the words up like a bucket drawing from a well and carefully placed the words into Her hands. I saw the emptiness of my heart when my siblings moved off to college, and my parents left me for their own pursuits. I saw the hopelessness cry out of me when I searched for someone to understand why or how my mind wandered into melancholic wastelands, but no one was there to answer. I saw my soul flatline as I cried out for meaning in the aftermath of rape, but couldn't seem to find it. I saw my physical body grow weary as I felt the weight of my brokenness slowly push me to the ground.

As I saw this last scene, I felt my whole body give way at the dumpster. I didn't have any more energy left in me. It felt like too much. I was tired of fighting. I was tired of being brave. I was tired of pressing on. I was tired of everything. I felt my tears roll down my face and fall to the ground. The Spirit noticed me and hugged me with Her presence. She gently reminded me that all was not lost; I had just run dry. Again, the words of Ezekiel filled the space around me, and I heard the echoes of Scripture: "I am going to open your graves and bring you up from them; I will bring you back . . . I will put my Spirit in you and you will live, and I will settle you in your land."[6] I felt my dry bones come to life. I looked around, and within the embrace of the Spirit, I stood on a brand new mountain, Mount Zion. I was perplexed at its majesty and my place there, yet I didn't ask questions. I just succumbed to its beauty. There was a peace, a calm joy, a serene holy moment where

---

5. Ezek 47:8–9.
6. Ezek 37:12–14.

## WEEK 6: GRACE—THE FINALITY OF DEATH

I watched the *me* I used to be drift away, and I stepped into the *me* I was meant to be. It felt magical, majestic, and surreal.

I whispered, *"Goodbye."* And that was it. That was when I finally, completely, surrendered.

Maybe this funeral, this surrender, was and is as simple as it sounds. It was a simple goodbye. I'm in the habit of overthinking things and thought this had to be a long process. I think that is why it took me so long to get to the other side. There always seemed to be a program, a process, a set of steps to accomplish to graduate. But, that's not how it was at Mount Zion. It was a wave of goodbye and turning to meet up with God.

During my drive to and from the dumpster every day, I would often hear a song on the radio that spoke about saying goodbye to all the lies we often believe about ourselves. And, like the song, I realized that even though my farewell was plain and simple, it was meant to be that way. So, to all those words the Spirit brought before me: regret, shame, alone, afraid, emptiness, and hopelessness: goodbye. I lay you to rest at the tomb. I know you will always be a memory, and you might come back in an ugly way again, but I will have no problem saying it again. Goodbye. I'm done fighting. I surrender.

Within the grace given to me, there is the finality of life. Freely given, freely available, freely absorbed. There is also the finality of death. Forever taken away, forever relinquished, forever cast out. I wouldn't have known what grace meant if it wasn't for this crazy notion of sitting in a place of hurt with God. I've sat in a place where He gives life and finalizes death. Two sides of the same coin.

I went to the dumpster yet another day and found out my days there were done. No other time, in the entire 40 days I had spent at the dumpster, had anyone been there. People had walked by, had approached, had waved, but no one ever came to take this space—except that last day. Curled up behind the green dumpster, labelled 4-8180, lay a man. He was sound asleep, with his backpack near his side. Homeless, broken, and in need of a place to lay his head, he found this place of refuge, this place of sanctuary. I went back to my van and sat in silence.

Three thoughts settled in my mind. First, I remembered the passage in the book of Matthew, "Whatever you did for one of the least of these brothers of mine, you did for me."[7] Let me be clear, I didn't feed, offer a drink, clothe, or even visit with this man. So, what did I do for this man? I gave him my spot. I gave him my place of belonging, healing, grace, death and resurrection. I received so much from Jesus on my journey, and this was one of the ways I could give back to Him. I decided that if I saw everyone around me, even the person in the mirror, as a place where God dwells, I would be able to give back to Him the life that He gave me. Everyone, this stranger included, became Jesus incarnate to me. Giving him my spot wasn't a transaction with God, nor was it a payment for Jesus' gift to me. It was a display of gratitude for my journey. I think I will visit this place from time to time to meet up with Jesus, and offer Him a breakfast sandwich, a cigarette perhaps, and a place to sit in silence.

The second thought that entered my mind was that Jesus had now fully, without a shadow of a doubt, taken my place literally and figuratively. God had been showing me during my exile that I wasn't ever truly alone. He kept telling me in a variety of ways how He was with me, that He shouldered my burdens, that He became me at the cross and gave of himself so I didn't have to. For no other reason except for love, he took all condemnation upon himself. For all the times that I had convinced myself that I deserved death, he was pointing out that my logic was usurped by His. And here at the dumpster, I was overcome by wonder because once again Jesus was in front of me, curled up on the concrete to show me He was ready to take this man's place too. No—that He already had taken his place. I hoped and prayed that even in his slumber, this man would be willing to absorb grace too.

My third thought was a tidal wave of relief that crashed over me. I knew I had crossed the Red Sea and had stepped onto the other side. I was walking down from all of the mountains into my new life.

---

7. Matt 25:40.

*You have not come to a mountain that can be touched and that is burning with fire; to darkness, gloom and storm; to a trumpet blast or to such a voice speaking words that those who heard it begged that no further word be spoken to them, because they couldn't bear what was commanded...*
*But you have come to Mount Zion, to the city of the living God, the heavenly Jerusalem. You have come to thousands upon thousands of angels in joyful assembly, to the church of the firstborn, whose names are written in heaven. You have come to God, the Judge of all, to the spirits of the righteous made perfect, to Jesus the mediator of a new covenant, and to the sprinkled blood that speaks a better word than the blood of Abel.*

THE AUTHOR OF HEBREWS[1]

---

1. Heb 12:18–20, 22–24.

# Bibliography

Cartwright, Mark. "Hades." *World History Encyclopedia,* last modified July 19, 2012. https://www.worldhistory.org/hades.

———. "Sisyphus." *World History Encyclopedia,* last modified December 14, 2016. https://www.worldhistory.org/sisyphus.

———. "Tantalus." *World History Encyclopedia,* last modified February 28, 2017. https://www.worldhistory.org/ Tantalus.

Contemplative Monk. "St. John of the Cross Quote." Facebook, accessed July 23, 2019. https://www.facebook.com/ContemplativeMonk/posts/in-the-inner-stillness-where-meditation-leads-the-spirit-secretly-anoints-the-so/1591118510937392.

Dickens, Charles. *1812–1879. A Christmas Carol and Other Stories.* New York: Modern Library, 1995.

Dictionary.com, s.v. "dis-." Accessed August 19, 2019. https://www.dictionary.com/browse/dis-.

Dictionary.com, s.v. "trans-." Accessed August 19, 2019. https://www.dictionary.com/browse/trans-.

Dilnawaz. "On This Day: Helen Keller Comprehends the Word 'Water.'" Dulcinea Media, Inc., April 5, 2012. https://www.findingdulcinea.com/news/on-this-day/march-april-08/on-this-day-helen-keller-comprehends-the-word-water/

"Enneagram Theory: Fixations (Habits of the Mind) — Melancholy." The Enneagram in Business, May 24, 2011. https://theenneagraminbusiness.com/theory/enneagram-theory-fixations-habits-of-mind-melancholy

Holcomb, Justin. "What is Grace?" Salem Web Network, August 15, 2019. https://www.christianity.com/theology/what-is-grace.html.

Jones, Tony. *Soul Shaper: Exploring Spirituality and Contemplative Practices in Youth Ministry.* Grand Rapids: Zondervan, 2003.

Lane, Beldon C. *The Solace of Fierce Landscapes.* Oxford: Oxford University Press, 1998.

Lexico.com, s.v. "melancholy (n.)." Accessed July 25, 2019. https://www.lexico.com/en/definition/melancholy.

MacLaren, Alexander. "Expositions of Holy Scripture." Accessed August 22, 2019. https://biblehub.com/commentaries/maclaren/john/1.htm.

# BIBLIOGRAPHY

Medrut, Flavia. "15 Most Enlightening Carl Jung Quotes." Goalcast Inc., January 23, 2023. https://www.goalcast.com/15-enlightening-carl-jung-quotes/

Norris, Kathleen. "Fighting the Noonday Demon: Kathleen Norris on Acedia, Boredom, and Desert Spirituality." The Table Podcast, February 28, 2018. http://cct.biola.edu/fighting-noonday-demon-kathleen-norris-acedia-boredom-desert-spirituality.

Nouwen, Henri. *Making All Things New: An Invitation to the Spiritual Life*. San Francisco: HarperOne, 1981.

Robinson, Robert. "Come Thou Fount of Every Blessing." *Psalter Hymnal*. Grand Rapids: Christian Reformed Church, 1987.

Rohr, Richard. "Grieving As Sacred Space." John Mark Ministries, January 3, 2003. https://www.jmm.org.au/articles/1266.htm

Taylor, Barbara Brown. *Learning to Walk in the Dark*. New York: HarperCollins, 2014.

www.ingramcontent.com/pod-product-compliance
Lightning Source LLC
Chambersburg PA
CBHW071742090426
42738CB00011B/2539